The Bedside Book of World History

An understandable overview of the human experience

Part 1: Prehistory to 1500
Part 2: 1500 to the Present

by Mike Maxwell

Maxwell Learning

First published in 2021 in the United States of America
by Maxwell Learning LLC, Mancos, Colorado

Copyright © 2021 by Michael G. Maxwell

All rights reserved

Graphics by the author.
Cover illustration from van Gogh's "The Bedroom,"
in the public domain: Creative Commons ID 537441

No part of this book may be reproduced or transmitted in any form or by any means without the written permission of the publisher except where permitted by law.

ISBN 978-1-7321201-4-3

Library of Congress Control Number: 2021900734

FIRST EDITION

FRONT COVER: Based on a detail from Vincent van Gogh's "The Bedroom," Arles, France, 1889, Art Institute of Chicago.

Regarding his use of color in this painting, van Gogh wrote his brother Theo, "I had wished to express utter repose with all these very different tones."

Contents

To the Reader	7
Recurring Dynamics of History	8

PART 1 : PREHISTORY TO 1500

1 Overview, Basics, Prehistory — 10

2 Ancient Mesopotamia and Egypt — 19
   Civilization is born in the Middle East

3 Ancient India and China — 28
   Civilization spreads east

4 Ancient Greece and Rome — 37
   Civilization spreads west

5 Early Middle Ages — 46
   500 to 1000 AD

6 Late Middle Ages — 56
   1000 to 1500

Part 2: 1500 to the Present

7	**1500s and 1600s** The Early Modern World	67
8	**1700s** Enlightenment and Revolution	77
9	**1800s** Industrialism and Imperialism	87
10	**1900 to 1950** World at War	97
11	**1950 to the Present** Cold War and Space Age	110
12	**Current Issues** A Changing World Order	118

Main topic index   128

To the Reader

Welcome to *The Bedside Book of World History*, which offers an overview of human development through time from prehistory to the present day. The reader may choose to delve into this story of human experience at any interesting point in the historical record, or to follow the narrative chronologically from past to present.

Unlike standard surveys of world history, this historical narrative recognizes knowledge that can be usefully applied in the future in the form of "Recurring Dynamics of History," which are described on the following page.

Two tools can help to make this story of human experience easier to grasp: large-scale maps that serve to orient the reader in space (such as the maps that begin each chapter) and a large-scale timeline that serves to orient the reader in time (such as the timeline depicted below).

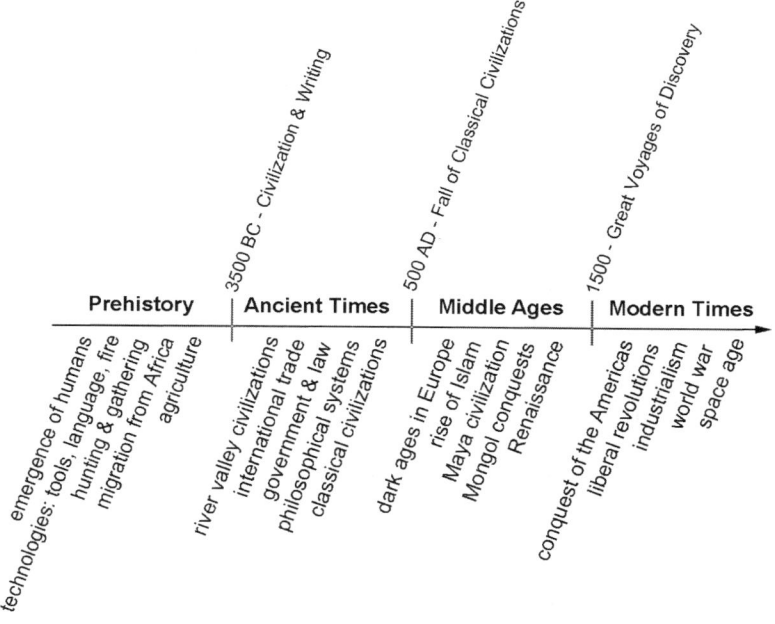

At the end of each chapter are a few open-ended questions meant to stimulate thinking about ideas presented in the chapter coupled with the reader's wider knowledge and personal experience. Often these questions call for an opinion, but, of course, opinions have little value without factual evidence to back them up, evidence that may be found between the covers of this book.

Recurring Dynamics of History

Although each historical event is unique in its details, a number of general patterns have repeated many times over the course of history. There is no guarantee that a pattern from the past will produce a similar result in the future, but past experience is usually the best indicator of future outcomes. We see this in our daily lives, where we routinely learn from past experience by repeating actions that were successful in the past and by avoiding actions that turned out to be mistakes.

Knowing about important recurring dynamics of history makes us smarter about human nature and the workings of the world, which can improve our judgment in human affairs and possibly help us and our leaders to avoid costly mistakes in the future. Several recurring dynamics of history are listed below. You might look for these dynamics—and others that you discover on your own—as you journey through the story of human experience presented in this book.

- Major cultures and empires have followed a general pattern of growth, flowering, and decline throughout history.

- Epidemic diseases have repeatedly claimed countless lives and altered human societies.

- Democracy is fragile; it has repeatedly fallen to authoritarian rulers.

- Humans exhibit a propensity to fear, dislike, kill, subjugate, and discriminate against people from groups different than their own.

- People tend to promote their self-interest and the interest of their group, so bias is all around us.

- Humans exhibit an instinct to exercise control over others, and humans exhibit a countervailing instinct to resist external control.

- Humans tend to position themselves along a political spectrum that ranges from conservative to liberal.

- Leaders often try to get their way by appealing to the emotions of their followers.

- Government actions tend to produce unintended consequences.

- Major events usually result from multiple causes, some long-term and some more immediate.

- Economies tend to be unstable and can malfunction if proper balance isn't maintained.

- Many or most military invasions of distant lands have failed over the long term.

- Those who promote war tend to disparage those who resist war as cowardly or unpatriotic.

- Powerful nations tend to prey on weaker nations.

- Rising powers have a tendency to go to war against established powers.

- Even superpowers experience limits to their power.

The Bedside Book of World History

Part 1
Prehistory to 1500

Chapter 1

A brief overview of world history, basic concepts of history and geography, and prehistory

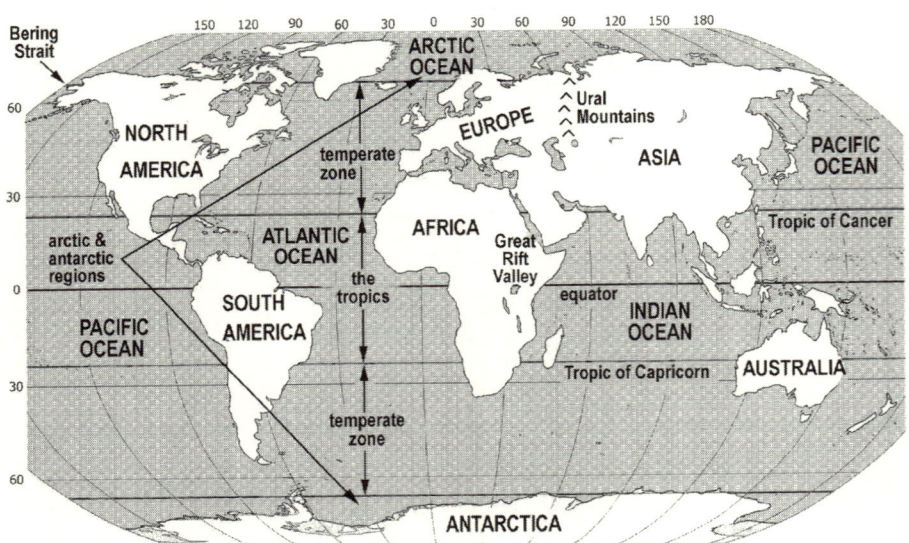

LOCATIONS: Europe, Asia, Africa, Antarctica, Australia, North America, South America, Ural Mountains, Pacific Ocean, Atlantic Ocean, Indian Ocean, Arctic Ocean, Great Rift Valley, Bering Strait, the tropics, arctic and antarctic regions, temperate zones

Preview

This chapter begins with a brief overview of human history that describes several great waves of change that swept over the world beginning in prehistoric times.

Then we will consider a few basic concepts of history and geography, which will be followed by a look at prehistory, the period of history when humans first appeared on the earth and before humans developed writing and civilization. We will see that humans invented agriculture near the end of prehistoric times, which prepared the way for civilization.

Chapter 1 – Overview, Basics, Prehistory

A brief overview of world history

World history is the story of human experience. It is a story of how people, ideas, and goods spread across the earth, creating our past and our present. To help us better understand this experience, we will divide history into four main eras: prehistory, ancient times, middle ages, and modern times. Our story begins during prehistory in east Africa, where human life apparently began. From Africa, humans spread to Eurasia (Europe and Asia), to Australia, and finally to the Americas. Early human migration was one of the great waves of history.

During most of history, most humans made their living by hunting and gathering. Then about 12,000 years ago, people in the Middle East learned how to cultivate a wild wheat plant, and agriculture was born—another great wave of history. No longer were humans constantly on the move searching for food. People could settle in one place, build cities, and invent tools like the plow, wheel, and writing. The complex societies that resulted are what we call civilization, another wave of history and the beginning of ancient times. In terms of a human lifetime, waves of change moved slowly, and much stayed the same amid the changes.

Waves of history were channeled over the earth by geography. The first civilizations arose in river valleys, where rivers provided fresh water for raising crops and transportation for moving crops to market. Beginning in Mesopotamia, civilization spread west to Egypt and east to India. These three civilizations formed an early international trading network that eventually extended across the connected lands of Eurasia and North Africa, a vast region that lies in a temperate climate zone where most of the world's people have lived since prehistoric times. More people meant more ideas, more inventions, and more diseases than in other parts of the world. Waves of change took longer to reach sub-Saharan Africa and the Americas because they were separated from Eurasia by physical barriers of desert and ocean.

As agriculture replaced hunting and gathering, human population increased. People in civilized societies divided themselves into unequal social classes with priests and kings at the top. Wealthy landowners collected rent payments from poor farmers, men came to dominate women, and slavery became common.

In the grasslands of central Eurasia, nomadic people chose not to settle down and raise crops. They lived by herding animals from pasture to pasture with the seasons. They learned to ride horses, developed cavalry skills, and attacked settled communities. Sometimes these nomadic raiders conquered great civilizations.

During ancient times people in Eurasia invented many things that still define civilization today, such as money, armies, iron, math, literature, democracy, and major world religions—to name a few. Ancient times lasted for roughly 4,000 years, ending about 500 AD after nomadic raiders brought down great classical civilizations in India, China, and the Mediterranean. The middle ages followed and lasted a thousand years.

Change spread to new places mostly through trading contacts. Some people welcomed change, while others avoided change and tried to maintain traditional ways. In the late middle ages, China was a superpower with the greatest navy in the world until China's rulers chose to reduce contact with the outside world and dismantled the fleet. This choice opened the door for Europeans to make the great voyages of discovery that connected the world and began modern times around the year 1500. Change was moving faster now.

Three centuries later, Europeans learned how to power machines by burning fuels, unleashing the Industrial Revolution—another great wave of history. Change moved even faster. At first, Europeans used their machines to dominate other peoples of the world who lacked advanced technology. Then Europeans turned their machines on each other, launching two suicidal world wars that ended European world dominance.

The stream of time flows on. As always, we humans face challenges to our survival, but in our time the challenges are global. Modern technology is consuming the world's resources, threatening the earth's environment, and it has produced weapons that could end all human life. The world is tied together through communications and trade, but the world remains divided between the "haves" and the "have nots."

History created our past and our present, but the future is up to us. There is no instruction manual for the future, but we do have a guide that can show us how the world works and how humans behave.

That guide is history.

Basic concepts of history and geography

primary and secondary sources

We learn about the past from historians. But where do historians get their information? Usually, they study primary sources, which are sources created at about the same time as the event being studied, often by people involved in the event. Examples of primary sources include artifacts uncovered by archeologists, art works, government records, diaries, letters, speeches, and newspaper articles.

Historians also study secondary sources. These are sources created after the event by people not involved in the event. Examples of secondary sources include history books, textbooks, encyclopedias, and the *The Bedside Book of World History*.

After historians examine their sources, they write histories based on their understanding of the truth. But, what they write may be influenced by their own opinions or by lack of information. It is not possible for historians to know everything about a past event, so they must rely on the evidence left behind in the form of primary and secondary sources. If new evidence is found, interpretations of history can change.

BC and AD

People in different parts of the world have adopted many ways to mark the passage of time. The Chinese calendar counts years from the reign of the mythical Yellow Emperor in 2698 BC. The Islamic calendar numbers years from 622 AD when Muhammad fled Mecca. Both calendars are based on lunar cycles. The year 2000 in our calendar is 4697 in the Chinese calendar and 1421 in the Islamic calendar.

Our solar-based calendar comes from ancient Egypt. It was modified by the Romans, and Europeans of the middle ages began to number years from the birth of Christ; years before year 1 were designated BC for "Before Christ," and years after year 1 were designated AD, an abbreviation for the Latin term Anno Domini, which means "in the year of the lord." This calendar has been adopted by most of the world for official purposes. AD years are counted forward from year 1; BC years are counted backward from year 1. Thus, 500 BC was earlier than 200 BC.

Those who wish to avoid the reference to Christ have begun using the term BCE (Before the Common Era) to replace BC, and CE (Common Era) to replace AD. The terms BCE and CE are found in some history books. This book uses the traditional terms BC and AD because they are more widely known in our culture, millions of historical documents bear these designations, there was no Common Era in history, and non-Christians may object to the suggestion that the Christian era is the "common era" of humankind.

hemispheres

A hemisphere is any half of earth's surface; the term comes from the Greek word for half a sphere. The equator (zero degrees latitude) divides the earth into the Northern Hemisphere and the Southern Hemisphere. The dividing line between the Eastern and Western Hemispheres is not so well defined, but it is usually placed at the Prime Meridian (zero degrees longitude) or at 20 degrees west longitude.

North and South America and surrounding waters are considered to be in the Western Hemisphere, while the continents of Europe, Africa, Asia, and Australia are considered to be in the Eastern Hemisphere.

climate zones

The earth has three main climate zones: the tropics, the temperate regions, and the arctic and antarctic regions. Although local climates can vary considerably within zones, the tropics are generally the warmest areas of the earth because they are near the equator, where the sun's rays are most direct. The Tropic of Cancer is an imaginary line that circles the earth at 23.5 degrees north latitude, the northernmost point reached by the sun during our summer (on the summer solstice). The Tropic of Capricorn lies at 23.5 degrees south latitude, the farthest point south reached by the sun during our winter (on the winter solstice).

The arctic and antarctic regions are located near the earth poles where the sun's rays are least direct and weakest: thus these are the coldest areas of the earth. The Arctic Circle is an imaginary line that circles the earth at 66.5 degrees north latitude; the Antarctic Circle lies at 66.5 degrees south latitude.

Those areas of the earth that lie between the tropics and the arctic/antarctic regions are called the temperate zones, those areas where temperature and climate tend to be more moderate. Most of Asia, Europe, and North America lie within the northern temperate zone, which is a good place to grow crops. This is where most of the world's human population has been concentrated since prehistoric times.

Prehistory: origins of the Earth and humans

Big Bang theory

Most astronomers agree that the universe probably began with an event similar to an explosion, a big bang. The universe is a term for all of outer space including the planets, stars, and galaxies. Galaxies are clusters of hundreds of millions of stars, and there are hundreds of millions of galaxies in the universe. Our world, Earth, is in the Milky Way galaxy, named after the milky-looking band of stars stretching across the night sky that is an edge-on view of our galaxy.

The Big Bang theory is supported by scientific observations that indicate galaxies in space are moving away from Earth. Astronomers use the speed of this movement to estimate the age of the universe at about 14 billion years. Many scientists accept a figure of about 5 billion years as the age of Earth.

Chapter 1 – Overview, Basics, Prehistory

continents

Geographers divide most of the land surface of the earth into seven large landmasses called continents. The continents are Europe, Asia, Africa, Antarctica, Australia, North America, and South America. Antarctica is the only continent not settled by humans. The Ural Mountains of Russia are considered the dividing line between Europe and Asia. Europe and Asia form a single large landmass called Eurasia.

The continents, however, cover less than a third of the earth's surface. Earth is mostly a water planet, and 97% of that water is found in the earth's four oceans, the Pacific, the Atlantic, the Indian, and the Arctic. Because ocean water is salty, it cannot be used for drinking, farming, or manufacturing. Far less than 1% of the earth's water is fresh water, water that is not salty and can be used to grow crops.

plate tectonics

According to the theory of plate tectonics, the earth's surface is composed of about a dozen plates of solid material that slowly move as they float on a bed of magma, or molten rock. In other words, the surface of the earth resembles a cracked eggshell, and the pieces of the shell are moving. These plates include both the ocean floor and the continents. The continents are simply high areas on the plates above sea level, so both the continents and the sea floor move with their plates.

Earthquakes and volcanoes often occur at boundaries between plates as the plates push together, spread apart, or slide against one another. For example, the Pacific Plate is slowly grinding past the North American Plate in California, creating enormous pressures along the San Andreas Fault that are expected to produce a major earthquake sometime within the next few decades. Plate tectonics continues to shape the earth's surface, as does erosion caused by wind and water. Scientists believe all of the present continents might have been together in a single large landmass long ago before they broke apart and drifted to their present locations on the earth. This supercontinent of the past is called Pangaea.

Great Rift Valley

This is a valley in eastern Africa where two of the earth's plates are spreading apart, exposing the fossil remains of early humans. Fossils are the remains of living organisms that have been left behind after the living tissue has slowly been replaced by stone-like material that preserves the form of the original organism. Scientists believe that the Great Rift Valley might be where human life began and spread to other areas of the earth, making humans the most widespread animal species in the world. If so, we are all Africans.

The Olduvai Gorge area of the Great Rift Valley has been the site of famous discoveries by the husband and wife team of Louis and Mary Leakey and other paleontologists. (Paleontologists are scientists who study the fossils of plants and animals.) Until the 1960s, it was thought that human life began in Asia until the Leakeys found older human fossils in Africa. Their son Richard Leakey has written: "Humans are unique because they have the capacity to choose what they do…The most obvious product of our hands and brains is technology. No other animal manipulates the world in the extensive and arbitrary way that humans do." (Technology is a term for inventions and tools that help us do things better or more easily.)

Australopithecus

Australopithecus was an extinct member of the hominid family, the family tree that includes modern humans. Australopithecus lived in Africa from about 4 to 1 million years ago. The first discovery of an early Australopithecus was made in the Great Rift Valley, the skeletal remains of a female now called Lucy.

Because Australopithecus walked on two feet and had a relatively large brain, it had human-like characteristics, but most scientists consider it to be prehuman. Walking upright was a big advantage; it gave Australopithecus a better view of the surrounding countryside, and it left both hands free to carry burdens and to use primitive tools and weapons. Australopithecus is Latin for "southern ape." (Many scientific terms in use today are derived from Latin, the language of the ancient Roman Empire.)

culture

Culture is a term for the knowledge and achievements passed on from one generation to another to form the way of life shared by a group of people. Most people living in Europe and North America share a common culture known as Western Civilization, also called Western culture or simply the West. The East refers to Asia, Asian culture, or Eastern Civilization. (This use does not correspond to the hemispheres.)

Human culture may have begun with Homo erectus, another extinct member of the hominid family, who lived from about two million to a half-million years ago. Homo erectus is Latin for "upright human." Homo erectus was the first hominid to hunt large animals and the first to leave Africa, migrating first to Asia and then to Europe. Homo erectus adapted to warm tropical climates and to freezing cold temperatures.

Evidence from archeology indicates that Homo erectus developed a culture that included the construction of shelters and the use of hand axes and fire and maybe spoken language. (Archeology is the scientific study of the remains of past human life and human activities.) Fire was powerful; it meant that humans could keep predators away, eat better by cooking their food, and extend their habitat into colder climates. If the definition of human is the ability to create new inventions, Homo erectus probably qualifies.

Perhaps the most important invention ever created by humans was spoken language. Language is a set of sounds that gives humans the capacity to communicate, cooperate, organize, and plan for the future.

Homo sapiens

This is the biological classification for modern humans. The earliest Homo sapiens were Neanderthals (Homo sapiens neanderthalensis) who developed about 150,000 years ago and went extinct shortly after encountering a human species with more advanced technology. The species that replaced Neanderthals was us, Homo sapiens sapiens. The term Homo sapiens is Latin for wise human.

From Africa, Homo sapiens spread over Eurasia and later reached Australia and America during the Ice Ages, when water locked in ice sheets lowered the level of oceans. Land exposed at the Bering Strait formed a "land bridge" where Asian peoples likely crossed to America while following wild game herds some 20,000 years ago. Others might have migrated to America from Europe along the edge of ice sheets.

These travelers became the Native Americans of North and South America, the last continents to be occupied by humans. The arrival of these skilled hunters was followed by a die-off of large animals including horses and camels. A strait is a narrow body of water connecting two larger bodies of water. The Bering Strait, 50 miles wide, connects the Pacific Ocean to the Arctic Ocean between Russia and Alaska.

Stone Age

History has been divided into three eras based on the kinds of tools, or technology, that people used during these periods: the Stone Age, the Bronze Age, and the Iron Age. By far the longest stretch of human history took place before and during the Stone Age, a period called prehistoric times, when people did not yet know how to read or write. The Stone Age began about 250,000 BC and ended about 4000 BC when the Bronze Age began in the Middle East. (These ages began at different times in different places.)

During the Stone Age, people learned to use fire and make stone tools and weapons; they also developed spoken language and farming. The earliest discoveries of human art are also from the Stone Age.

Paleolithic is a scientific term applied to the early Stone Age, when humans made their living mostly by hunting, scavenging, or gathering wild food such as nuts and berries. Neolithic means the late Stone Age, when agriculture began, and copper tools were developed. (*Neo* means "new," *lithic* means "stone," terms that come from Greek, another ancient language that contributed to the modern language we use today.)

Some questions to consider:

Can we ever be sure we know the absolute truth about a historical event?

What kinds of things change throughout human history, and what kinds of things stay pretty much the same?

Can knowledge of the past be helpful in living our lives in the present and future? If so, how?

Is it possible to derive lessons or principles from history that might help people to make better decisions in the future?

Chapter 2

Ancient Mesopotamia and Egypt: Civilization is born in the Middle East

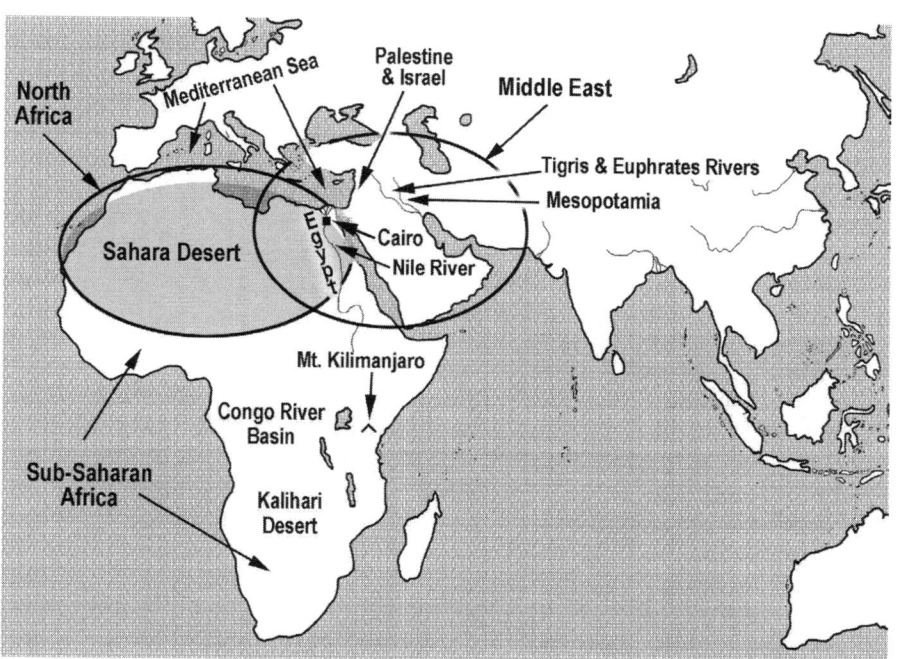

LOCATIONS: Middle East, Mesopotamia, Tigris and Euphrates Rivers, Israel, Palestine, Mediterranean Sea, Sahara Desert, sub-Saharan Africa, North Africa, Egypt, Nile River, Cairo

Preview

The next three chapters will visit major early civilizations of *ancient times* (about 3500 BC to 500 AD), the period of history when human civilization began. The earliest civilizations developed in river valleys because these were good places to grow crops—and it was agriculture that made civilization possible. We begin in the Middle East with the first-known civilization, which arose in Mesopotamia (now Iraq), and then we'll journey to the fascinating land of ancient Egypt.

agriculture

Before the Neolithic period, most humans made their living by hunting and gathering, which meant that humans were constantly on the move following wild game herds. This began to change about 12,000 years ago, when people in the Middle East discovered that they could plant and harvest a wheat plant they found growing wild. At about the same time, people began to domesticate wild animals, raising them for food and as a source of power that could pull wagons and plows. (Agriculture means farming and raising livestock.)

People no longer had to follow the wandering animal herds; they could settle in one place, grow crops, and eventually build towns and cities. With permanent homes, people could collect more possessions, which encouraged the invention of new technologies such as pottery making and looms for weaving. Because agriculture could support more people per square mile than hunting and gathering, human population jumped from about two million people during the early Stone Age to about 60 million during the late Stone Age.

Farmers learned to grow more food than they needed for their own use, resulting in a surplus. Agricultural surpluses made it possible to accumulate wealth, and they led to job specialization because not everyone had to raise food to make a living. Some people could specialize in nonagricultural work—like making pottery, or becoming priests or government officials—and be supported by others from the agricultural surplus. Agriculture became the main source of wealth in most societies until the industrial age.

Jericho (JAIR-uh-koe)

Agriculture and irrigation began in an area of the Middle East called the Fertile Crescent. Villages grew near farmlands, and the world's first known city developed at Jericho in Palestine around 8000 BC. Walls were built around Jericho to protect its agricultural surplus from nomadic raiders. Warfare, too, might have begun at Jericho. Agriculture later developed independently in China and in the Americas.

Hunting and gathering declined as agriculture became the way most humans made their living. Agriculture and other technologies spread fastest in Eurasia for several reasons: Much of Eurasia lies in a temperate zone suitable for agriculture; Eurasia had more plants and animals that could be raised by humans, and it had more people. Diseases, which often come from contact with animals, spread fastest in Eurasia too.

civilization

Agriculture made civilization possible because it permitted humans to settle permanently in one place, build cities, and develop complex societies. Large groups of people living together encouraged job specialization, the development of government, and written language, all of which are important features of civilization. Writing probably began as a way to record business dealings, especially the exchange of agricultural products. Cities and writing are often considered the primary indicators of civilization. When people started to write, prehistoric times ended, and historic times began.

Not everything about civilization was positive. Complex societies usually meant greater separation of people into classes based on social position or wealth. Often a wealthy class of aristocrats controlled the land and collected rents from poor farmers. Society became divided between the "haves" and the "have nots." Civilized societies may have been more patriarchal (male dominated) than hunter-gatherer bands in which everyone helped to supply food that ensured the group's survival.

the Middle East

The Middle East is a popular term for a region that includes southwest Asia and northeast Africa, extending from Libya in the west to Afghanistan in the east. The terms Near East or Southwest Asia are sometimes used to identify parts of this region. We can trace Western culture back to the beginnings of civilization in the Middle East. It was also the birthplace of three major world religions, Judaism, Christianity, and Islam. Today the Middle East is important as the major oil-producing region of the world and as a hot spot of international tension including the Arab-Israeli conflict and two recent wars fought by the United States against Iraq.

Mesopotamia

Located in the modern country of Iraq, Mesopotamia is known as the "cradle of civilization" because it is here that civilization first began around 3500 BC, a date considered the beginning of ancient times. Mesopotamia is a region, not a country, within the larger region of the Middle East. Regions are basic units of geography. A region is an area of the earth with consistent cultural or physical characteristics. Regions may be large like the Middle East, or they may be smaller like Mesopotamia.

Mesopotamia lies between the Tigris and Euphrates Rivers; the name Mesopotamia means "between the waters" in Greek. Here farmers learned to build irrigation systems that turned the dry valley into a prosperous center of agriculture supporting many people. This is an early example of how humans can change the natural environment.

As settlements in southern Mesopotamia grew into busy cities, this area, called Sumer, became the world's first civilization. The Sumerians built walled cities and developed the earliest-known writing called cuneiform, in which scribes (record-keepers) carved symbols onto wet clay tablets that were later dried. The Sumerians are credited with writing the world's oldest story, the *Epic of Gilgamesh,* about the life of a Sumerian king. The Sumerian number system was based on 12, which explains why we have 60-minute hours, 24-hour days, 12-month years, and 360-degree circles.

religion

We can find the beginnings of religion in Neanderthal burials that included food and tools, presumably for use in the afterlife. Religion may have begun as a way to cope with misfortune and with the human awareness of death. Early religions usually worshiped several gods, a practice called polytheism.

Religion was extremely important in Sumer, where priests were originally the most powerful people in society. Later, warrior kings would take control. Priests supervised the worship of seven great gods: earth, sky, sun, moon, saltwater, freshwater, and storm. Sumerians believed their gods lived in statues housed in temples including large pyramid-like structures called ziggurats. Priests fed the god statues daily.

Code of Hammurabi

Because the fertile valley of Mesopotamia had no natural barriers for protection, its wealth attracted many raiders and conquerors over the centuries. Civilizations came and went amid much warfare. One of the most powerful civilizations to arise in Mesopotamia was Babylon (1900 to 500 BC).

Hammurabi was an early king of Babylon who created an empire by bringing much of Mesopotamia under his control. (An empire is a collection of states [countries] controlled by one government.) Hammurabi helped unite the Babylonian Empire by publishing a set of laws known as the Code of Hammurabi, history's first known written laws. He had the 300 laws of the code carved on stone pillars for all to see, which meant that nobody was above the law; it applied to everyone. The goals of Hammurabi's Code included "stable government and good rule...that the strong may not oppress the weak."

Babylon later became known for its hanging gardens, one of the Seven Wonders of the Ancient World, and for the decadent lifestyle of its people; "a Babylon" now means a place of corruption and sin. The Bible mentions the Tower of Babel, probably a ziggurat, that the builders hoped would reach to heaven. In response to their arrogance, God confused the builders' language so they could no longer understand one another's speech. The Bible says this is how the people of the world came to "babble" in different languages.

Hebrews

The Hebrews were an ancient people of the Middle East who established the kingdom of Israel at the eastern end of the Mediterranean Sea about 1000 BC. There they founded the religion of Judaism. Judaism was unusual because it worshipped only one God (monotheism). It was also a universal religion that could be worshipped anywhere; it was not tied to a particular place like the gods of Sumer.

The Israelites were conquered by the Babylonians in the 500s BC and taken to Babylon in chains. During the exile in Babylon, Jewish scribes began to write the Bible in an effort to preserve Hebrew culture and religion. Laws contained in the Bible such as "An eye for an eye, and a tooth for a tooth" have a basis in the Code of Hammurabi. (The Jewish Bible is what Christians call the Old Testament.) Over the centuries since then, Jews have settled in many parts of the world, but they have maintained their identity as a people.

In an effort to regain their ancient homeland in the Middle East, Jews took over Arab lands in Palestine after World War II to create the modern nation of Israel, which resulted in years of conflict between Jews and Arabs that still continues.

Bronze Age

The Stone Age was followed by the Bronze Age, when people learned to make bronze tools, ornaments, and weapons. Bronze is made by combining copper with tin, which produces a harder metal than copper alone, and it holds an edge much longer. The Bronze Age was a time of great invention; the wheel, plow, writing, money, cities, armies, and chariots all came into use during the Bronze Age in Mesopotamia.

The Bronze Age is important in history as the period when civilization and writing began, marking the end of prehistoric times and the beginning of ancient times. In Mesopotamia, the Bronze Age lasted from roughly 4000 BC to the beginning of the Iron Age around 1000 BC.

Egypt

Not long after the world's first civilization arose between the Tigris and Euphrates Rivers in Mesopotamia, civilization spread west to the Nile River valley of Egypt. Egyptians probably learned about irrigation, the plow, writing, and other technologies from Mesopotamia.

Egypt is said to be a "gift of the Nile" because the river provided irrigation water, fertile soils due to annual floods, and easy transportation by boat. Boats on the Nile were pulled north by the Nile's current, and they sailed south with the prevailing winds. Egyptians considered the river sacred; it separated the "land of the living" on the east bank (where the sun rises) from the "land of the dead" on the west bank (where the sun sets).

Egypt's two main geographic features are the Nile and the Sahara Desert. Ancient Egypt was a long, narrow oasis along the river in the desert. It has been said, "geography is destiny," and perhaps this was true in Egypt, where the Nile was the lifeblood of the country, and the desert provided natural barriers to enemies permitting ancient Egyptian civilization to last for 3,000 years, the longest in history (3100 BC to 30 BC).

Ancient Egyptians had a polytheistic religion; their important gods included Ra, god of the sun and creator of life, and Osiris, god of rebirth. The struggle between Osiris and his evil brother, Set, represented the eternal struggle between good and evil.

Many works of art, literature, and architecture survive from ancient Egypt including huge tombs of the pharaohs, the Sphinx, and the great pyramids near Cairo, Egypt's modern-day capital city. The ancient Egyptians also developed a 365-day calendar based on the solar year. Their calendar was adopted by the Roman Empire and became the calendar we use today.

pharaohs

Pharaohs were the rulers of ancient Egypt who were worshipped as gods. Their wealth came from the bountiful agriculture made possible by the Nile. Egypt's pharaohs controlled strong central governments that built massive public works such as the irrigation systems that tamed the Nile's floods, allowing agriculture to flourish in the desert. Notable among Egypt's pharaohs were Ramses II (Ramses the Great) who successfully defended Egypt from attacks by the mysterious "Sea Peoples," and he is known for building great temples and statues. Queen Hatshepsut was the first important woman ruler in history, and Cleopatra was the last queen of the thirty-one dynasties, or ruling families, of Egypt.

The best-known pharaoh is Tutankhamen, or King Tut, who died at the age of eighteen. Although his reign was not very important, he became famous in our time for the discovery of his unplundered tomb in the 1920s, the only tomb of a pharaoh found intact. Grave robbers looted the other tombs centuries ago. Although Tutankhamen was a minor king, his tomb contained fantastic riches: over 5,000 objects in four rooms including a spectacular lifelike mask of solid gold that covered the head and shoulders of his mummy (his preserved body). King Tut's tomb is one of the most impressive archeological discoveries of all time.

government

As societies grew larger, government became necessary to provide an orderly way to make decisions, to maintain public order through police and courts, and to supply services that were not provided by merchants. In the hot Egyptian desert, for example, lack of water could mean starvation and death. Only government could ensure that all farmers received their fair share of water and that all farmers maintained their ditches so irrigation systems did not break down.

Today, governments still maintain public water systems, and they perform other functions not provided by business such as national defense and education. Major types of governments in history have included monarchies (kings & queens) based on rule by a royal family or dynasty, democracies based on rule by the people, and dictatorships in which one person takes control of a nation, usually with help from the military.

pyramids

Ancient Egyptians were preoccupied with religion and the afterlife. The status of priests in Egyptian society was just below that of pharaohs. For a person to enter the next life, the body had to be preserved through mummification and religious rituals performed by priests. Skilled embalmers prepared the body by removing the vital organs, then drying and wrapping the body in strips of linen. Eventually, ordinary Egyptians were mummified, and archeologists have even discovered an ancient Egyptian cemetery filled with mummified cats. All Egyptians, including pharaohs, had an incentive for doing good during their lives; the Egyptian religion held that good works were necessary to enter the afterlife.

The most famous burial tombs of ancient Egypt are the great pyramids at Giza near Cairo. These and other tombs were built to house the bodies of pharaohs for the afterlife. The pyramids are the oldest and the only remaining examples of the Seven Wonders of the Ancient World. Without iron tools or wheeled vehicles, workers cut, moved, and lifted millions of limestone blocks weighing an average of 2.5 tons each. Archeologists believe that the workers who built the pyramids were not slaves but valued members of society who lived in a nearby community with their families. Standing guard over the pyramids at Giza is the Sphinx, a great rock sculpture with the head of a pharaoh and the body of a lion. The age of pyramid building in Egypt lasted from about 2700 BC to 1000 BC.

hieroglyphics

This was the ancient Egyptian system of writing that used pictures to represent words or syllables. Hieroglyphics preserved records of ancient Egyptian culture for thousands of years. Egyptians carved hieroglyphics into stone, and they wrote on papyrus made from a reed plant that was pressed and dried to make a paper-like material. Paper gets its name from papyrus. Papyrus was rolled into scrolls, which made written records lightweight, compact, and portable.

Modern people did not understand Egyptian hieroglyphics until the Rosetta Stone was discovered in Egypt by Napoleon's armies in the late 1700s. Carved into the Rosetta Stone was a message written in hieroglyphics along with a translation in Greek. Modern scholars understood Greek and used it to break the code of hieroglyphics. Now we can read about details of life in ancient Egypt from love poems to surgical procedures. A "Rosetta Stone" has come to mean the key to understanding a difficult problem.

Africa

Egypt is in the northeast corner of Africa, which is the second-largest continent after Asia. Africa's major geographic features include the Sahara Desert in the north, the Kalahari Desert in the south, and tropical rain forests centered on the Congo River basin in south-central Africa. In eastern Africa are the Great Rift Valley, the Nile River, and Africa's highest mountain, Mt. Kilimanjaro. The savanna is a large land area in central and southeast Africa with grasslands and scattered trees. The savanna is home to many of the famed, large wild animals of Africa including lions, giraffes, and elephants.

The Nile is the longest river in the world. It originates in the highlands of central Africa and flows north for more than 4,000 miles to the Mediterranean Sea, where it forms a wide triangle-shaped delta in northern Egypt. Deltas are flat areas of land that sometimes form at the mouths of rivers where the rivers deposit sediment as they flow into the sea. Because of their abundant wildlife and plant life, deltas have always attracted humans. Egypt's two largest cities, Cairo and Alexandria, are on the Nile River delta.

Sahara Desert

The Sahara Desert is about the size of the United States, which makes it the largest dry desert in the world. It extends from the Atlantic Ocean on the west to the Red Sea on the east, and it is still expanding to the south. The Sahara separates North Africa from sub-Saharan Africa. North Africa borders the Mediterranean Sea and includes the Sahara and lands lying to the north of the desert including the Atlas Mountains and the modern countries of Morocco, Algeria, Tunisia, Libya, and Egypt.

Sub-Saharan Africa is the land that lies south of the desert. It has sometimes been called "black Africa" because people living there have darker skins than North Africans. Dark skin appears to be an adaptation to climate. People living in the tropics need more skin pigment to protect them from intense rays of the sun, while people living closer to the earth's poles have paler skins to absorb more sunlight. People with black skins also live near the equator in India and Australia. It's been estimated that it took roughly 20,000 years for skin color to change from black to white as humans spread north out of Africa.

Some questions to consider:

Can civilizations exist without governments to maintain control?

Are modern people smarter than ancient people, or do we just have better technology?

Is geography destiny?

In this chapter, we saw evidence that some governments and religions in ancient societies encouraged their people to be good and fair to each other. Do we see similar evidence in our society?

Chapter 3

Ancient India and China: Civilization spreads east

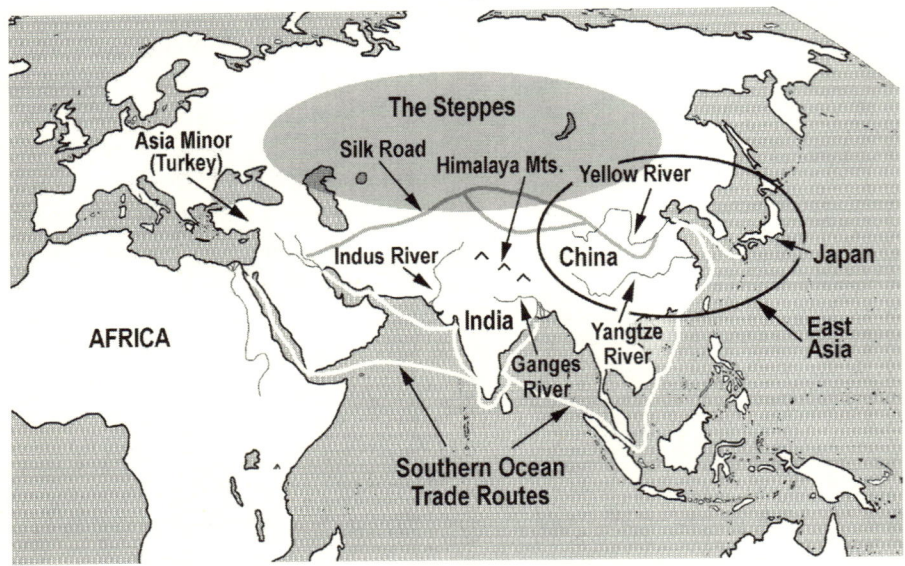

LOCATIONS: India, China, Japan, Asia Minor (Turkey), East Asia, Indus River, Yellow River, the Steppes, Silk Road, southern ocean trade routes, Himalaya Mountains.

Preview

After the world's first major civilizations arose in the Middle East, trade and civilization spread eastward to the Indus River valley of India. India was the birthplace of two major world religions, Hinduism and Buddhism, and India is the source of our zero-based numbering system. India would become the hub of a large trading network that extended from Europe all the way to China.

China, the world's fourth early civilization, also began in a river valley: the Yellow River valley of northern China. After China expanded south to the Yangtze River valley, the land between the two rivers became China's heartland, known as the "Middle Kingdom." After a ruthless emperor took control of China, it became the superpower of Asia.

28

Asia

Asia is the world's largest continent, sharing the landmass of Eurasia with Europe. The Ural Mountains of Russia are considered the dividing line between Asia and Europe. Asia was the site of three of the world's earliest civilizations, in Mesopotamia, India, and China. Today Asia has three-fifths of the world's population and the two most populous countries in the world, China and India. Because Asia is so huge, geographers have divided Asia into several regions. On the western side of Asia is the Middle East, which includes Asia Minor (present-day Turkey). Farther east is central Asia. To the south lies the Indian subcontinent. On the eastern side of Asia are East Asia (sometimes called the Far East) and Southeast Asia.

India

Most of the country of India is a triangular-shaped peninsula that juts into the Indian Ocean. Due to its central location on the Indian Ocean between China and the Middle East, India became the ancient world's largest trading center. India also gave the world important new ideas, including the numbering system we use today and the religions of Hinduism and Buddhism. Today India is the second most populous country in the world after China, and India is the world's largest democracy. The capital of India is New Delhi. India and nearby countries form a region known as the Indian subcontinent, or Southern Asia.

After civilization first emerged in Mesopotamia and Egypt, it spread east to India. The earliest civilization in India grew along the Indus River valley of western India (now Pakistan) around 2500 BC. The Indus Valley Civilization had a written language and large cities with sophisticated plumbing systems. These were the first people to grow cotton. Ships and overland trade caravans connected India to Mesopotamia and Egypt in an early international trading network. The Indus Valley Civilization lasted for about a thousand years before it went into decline, possibly due to climate change that brought cooler and dryer weather.

caste system

Under ancient India's caste system, people were born into permanent classes for life, and they could marry only within their own caste. There were four main castes with complicated rules of behavior: (1) the priests, (2) the warriors, (3) the merchants, and (4) the common people, mostly peasants and laborers. Most people of ancient India were members of the commoner class, which had limited rights.

A fifth group, the Untouchables, was outside the caste system. Considered not fully human, Untouchables performed the worst jobs such as skinning animals, cleaning toilets, and burying the dead.

While the caste system may seem unfair to us today, it provided a means for different kinds of people to live together peacefully while avoiding the slavery common to many ancient cultures. Although discrimination based on caste has been outlawed in India for decades, it still influences what kind of jobs people can get and whom they will marry.

Hinduism

Hinduism is the oldest major religion in the world today; it survived so long by changing and adjusting to new circumstances. To Hindus, all religions are acceptable, and the practices of other religions may be included as part of Hindu worship. Hindus believe in an eternal and infinite spiritual principle called Brahman that is the ultimate reality and foundation of all existence. Brahman can take the form of many gods, including Brahma the creator of the universe, Vishnu the preserver, and Shiva the destroyer.

For Hindus, a proper life is unconcerned with worldly riches; the goal is to seek union with Brahman, a quest that may take many lifetimes. Hindus believe in reincarnation, meaning that the soul never dies and may be reborn again in a different body. Karma, all of the actions of a person's life, will determine if a person returns in the next life at a higher level on the ladder of incarnation and closer to union with Brahman.

Hinduism is the largest religion of India and a defining feature of Indian culture. Hinduism and the caste system served to maintain order among India's many ethnic groups because each person knew his or her place in society, and people who followed the rules could hope to move to a higher caste in the next life.

Buddhism

Not everyone in India was satisfied with Hinduism. In the 500s BC, a young Hindu prince raised in luxury became troubled by the suffering he saw in the world. He left his wife and infant son to become a wandering monk, seeking a way to end the suffering. After six years of solitary searching, he found an answer and began to teach. His followers called him the "Buddha," or "the enlightened one."

Buddha taught that our life in the physical world is merely an illusion. When people let go of their worldly pain and worries, they can unite with the universal soul and achieve a state of complete peace called nirvana. Like Hindus, Buddhists believe nothing is permanent, that life constantly moves through cycles of birth, death, and rebirth like the turning of a wheel. Although Buddha accepted the Hindu belief in reincarnation, he taught that people could achieve nirvana from their actions in this life alone, and he rejected the caste system. For these reasons, Buddhism became popular among the lower classes in India.

Today Buddhism is a major world religion. Although it began in India, Buddhism spread to the east and declined in India as Buddhism was absorbed into Hinduism. Buddhists are now found in the greatest numbers in East Asia and Southeast Asia.

Ashoka

Centuries after the Indus Valley Civilization died, cities and civilization arose again farther to the east in the fertile Ganges River valley. India was torn by warfare between kingdoms until the first Indian empire was established in the Ganges valley by the Mauryan Dynasty in 324 BC. Its greatest leader was Ashoka, who extended his empire to the south in a bloody invasion that conquered all but the southern tip of India.

Then Ashoka had a sudden change of heart. He publicly announced his grief at the suffering caused by his armies, and he rejected violence. He even gave up hunting and eating meat. Ashoka converted to Buddhism, and he spread Buddhist thinking throughout India and to neighboring countries. Ruling India with Buddhist ideals, Ashoka's government promoted the welfare of the people by kind acts such as digging new wells, building hospitals for people and animals, allowing freedom of religion, and easing harsh laws.

Ashoka also encouraged long-distance ocean trade. It was during his reign that India became the center of a vast, southern ocean-trading network that stretched from China to Africa and the Middle East.

Gupta Empire

Historians consider the Mauryan Empire and the Gupta Empire that followed (in the 300s and 400s AD) to be the greatest civilizations of India's classical period, a period when India underwent great cultural and political advancement. The reign of the Gupta Empire has been called India's "golden age," a high point of Indian history when art, drama, literature, and science flourished.

Gupta mathematicians invented the zero, an amazing number with no value that gives value to the place of other numbers. The zero made it possible to calculate numbers faster and more accurately, and it was adopted the world over. Doctors developed an inoculation against smallpox. Farmers learned how to turn the juice from sugarcane into dried sugar crystals that could be easily stored and traded over long distances. Cotton from India clothed people across much of the ancient world. Gupta India was a land of wonders.

The Gupta Empire declined in the early 500s AD when tribes of nomadic horsemen called Huns invaded from grasslands to the north, but the cultural patterns that developed during India's classical period created a vital culture in Southern Asia that endures to this day.

nomadic raiders

People of ancient times developed four basic patterns for making a living. Some were still hunters and gatherers stalking wild game herds, but most people lived in farming villages. Another group lived in cities supported largely by wealth from agriculture. A fourth group lived in pastoral societies; these were nomadic herders of the grasslands who did not settle down in one place like farmers. They moved their domesticated (tame) animals—sheep, goats, cows, horses, and camels—from pasture to pasture with the seasons.

Pastoral people were mobile, and they developed military tactics to protect their animals from thieves. Pastoral nomads of the steppes (grasslands of central Eurasia) became skilled at using horses in warfare, and they sometimes raided settled communities. These were the nomadic raiders who attacked Jericho, Sumer, the Gupta Empire, and others. Many governments of Eurasia began with nomads sweeping in from the steppes and taking control. Centuries of warfare between nomadic raiders and civilized peoples in Eurasia led to advancements in military organization and technology unmatched elsewhere in the world.

China

The world's fourth great, early civilization also got its start along a river valley, the Yellow River of northeastern China, where farmers grew millet and wheat. Farming later moved south to the Yangtze (YONG-zuh) river, where rice production led to an increase in China's population. The land between the rivers became the center of Chinese civilization, the so-called Middle Kingdom. Early Chinese culture grew in relative isolation due to physical barriers and long distances that separated it from other major civilizations of Eurasia. The world's highest mountain range, the Himalayas, separates China from India.

The Chinese have long believed in a philosophy that recognizes a fundamental balance in nature between opposite but complimentary principles called yin and yang. Examples include day/night, hot/cold, wet/dry, and male/female. Central to Chinese philosophy and religion is a belief that people should avoid extremes and seek harmony with the balance of nature. (A philosophy is a system of basic beliefs about life.)

With nearly one-fourth of the world's population, China today is the world's most populous country, and it has a fast-growing economy. China was a superpower in the past, and it has become a superpower again in this century. China and its neighboring countries of Mongolia, Korea, and Japan form a region bordering the Pacific Ocean known as East Asia or the Far East.

mandate from heaven

The Zhou (JOH) dynasty took control of China in 1122 BC and ruled for nearly 900 years. To give their government legitimacy, Zhou and later Chinese rulers claimed to rule with approval from the gods, a mandate from heaven. Although this claim was meant to enhance the emperor's authority, it also established the right to overthrow an ineffective emperor. The emperor was expected to protect his people by ruling in a way that pleased the gods. If trouble developed in the empire—droughts or military defeats, for example—people might say the emperor had lost his mandate from heaven, and the emperor could be overthrown.

Over many centuries, China's history experienced a recurring pattern. A ruling dynasty would start out strong and gradually weaken over time until it was replaced by a new dynasty. Then the pattern would repeat.

Zhou rulers controlled their kingdom through a feudal system, meaning that they divided the land into smaller territories and appointed officials to govern them. When the Zhou dynasty eventually weakened, some of these territories developed into strong states that opposed the emperor and began fighting among themselves. These bloody conflicts lasted for over two centuries, a time called the Warring States period.

Confucius

Confucius was born in 551 BC, when Zhou rulers were losing control of their empire. He tried to return harmony to China with a philosophy based on devotion to the family, respect between the classes, high moral ideals, and learning. He emphasized individual duty and responsibility, what we might call a strong work ethic. The family was the center of Confucian society, with the father at the head. The mother and children owed total obedience to the father. Family ancestors were honored and not forgotten.

Confucius promoted an orderly society in which people of higher rank were courteous to those below, and those of lower rank were respectful to those above. Confucius said a ruler should act like a good father and lead by example, not through power and harsh laws. "When the ruler does right, all men will imitate his self-control."

While the teachings of Confucius were not very influential in his lifetime, they soon became a guiding philosophy of Chinese civilization, and they still exert a strong influence on Chinese culture today.

The First Emperor

One of China's warring states, the Qin (CHIN) kingdom of western China, grew wealthy from agriculture based on extensive irrigation. With this wealth, the Qin ruler raised a powerful army and spent twenty years ruthlessly conquering China's warring states. He declared himself First Emperor in 221 BC. Thus, it was the First Emperor, Qin Shi Huangdi, who brought China under a central government and gave China its name.

To unify China, the First Emperor stripped the regional warlords of their power, and he forced them to move to the capital where he could control them. He also standardized the Chinese language, money, roads, and weights and measures. The First Emperor ruled with a philosophy that considered people selfish and evil by nature; he adopted strict laws and harsh punishments to keep people in line. He also tried to control what people could think; it is said that he buried scholars alive, burned books including the teachings of Confucius, and brutally eliminated those who disagreed with him.

Great Wall of China

Natural barriers protected China on three sides: oceans to the east and south, mountains and desert to the west. But China's northern border lay open to attack from Huns. The First Emperor ordered a number of individual walls joined together to form one great stone wall to defend China's northern border from attack. Hundreds of thousands of laborers worked on the Great Wall for years, and many workers died under the harsh conditions. Gates in the wall became centers of trade with the nomadic peoples who lived outside. The Great Wall was repaired and rebuilt a number of times over the centuries, and parts of it still stand.

The First Emperor also built for himself a magnificent underground tomb, and nearby he buried a terra-cotta army of life-size soldiers to protect him for eternity. (Terra-cotta is the brownish-orange pottery used today to make flowerpots.) One pit contained sculptures of 6,000 infantrymen (foot soldiers), and a second pit held the cavalry (mounted soldiers) complete with life-size horses, all arranged in battle formation. One of the great archeological finds of the 20th century, the terra-cotta army was uncovered accidentally in 1974 by a farmer digging a well.

Hoping to find a way to avoid death, the First Emperor experimented with a number of potions until he killed himself by accidental poisoning. The Qin Dynasty lasted for only fifteen years, but it began a Chinese tradition of strong central governments controlled by powerful rulers.

Han Dynasty

The harsh rule of the First Emperor was so unpopular that the Qin Dynasty was overthrown shortly after the emperor's death. Following a period of civil war, the Han Dynasty took control of China in 206 BC. Han rulers adopted Confucian ideas about creating a respectful and orderly society, and they set up a civil service system to run the government with well-educated officials chosen by written tests.

The Han Dynasty expanded China's empire to the south and west, and it produced marvels that would change the world, including the ship's rudder, the magnetic compass, and paper. The four-hundred-year reign of the Han Empire was so successful that it is considered the greatest of China's classical dynasties.

The Han Empire eventually weakened, fell apart, and was replaced by three kingdoms in 220 AD. About a hundred years later, Hun invaders took control of the Chinese heartland. The period of classical civilization in China was over, but the Chinese were left with an enduring belief that China was the center of civilization.

Silk Road

During the Han Dynasty, regular trade began over the Silk Road, actually a network of trails that stretched 4,000 miles from China to the Roman Empire. Only the Chinese knew how to raise silkworms and weave silk; Chinese silk was worth its weight in gold in Rome. Europeans also acquired a taste for other Asian luxury goods including spices, a taste that would later send Columbus on his voyages of discovery.

The Silk Road was a two-way street. Asian goods were traded for Western goods, which flowed back along the Silk Road to China. Imports from the west to China included gold, silver, powerful horses, new foods, and Buddhism. This overland trade was made possible by the camel, the "ship of the desert," with its large padded feet for walking on shifting desert sands and its ability go long distances without food or water.

Trade routes such as the Silk Road were pioneered by nomads. For a price, nomads provided caravans with pack animals and protection. The Silk Road in the north joined with the southern ocean shipping routes to form a trading web that spread goods, technologies, and ideas between Asia, Europe, and North Africa.

Iron Age

Advanced Bronze Age civilizations of the eastern Mediterranean and Middle East collapsed around 1200 BC following attacks from a group of raiders known as the "Sea Peoples." Little is known about where the Sea Peoples came from and what caused them to move into new territories, but disruption of the bronze trade led to a transformation to a newer metal technology, iron.

This is when people learned how to use a draft of air from a furnace or bellows to produce the hot temperatures needed to melt iron from iron ore and to shape it into tools and weapons. Iron was much stronger than bronze, and it was less expensive because iron ore was easier to find than the tin needed to make bronze. Iron working not only meant better tools and weapons, it meant many more of them, a major technological change.

After iron working began in the Middle East, it spread to India and to much of the civilized world. Iron had a big impact on agriculture and warfare. Iron plow blades and hoes made it possible to work heavier soils than before, extending agriculture into new lands and boosting human populations. Armies grew bigger and deadlier due to more effective and less expensive iron weapons and armor. There is no definite ending date for the Iron Age, but people today might say we live in the "Industrial Age" or the "Digital Age."

Some questions to consider:

If you were sent on a mission to establish a new civilization on a distant planet similar to earth, where would you locate your civilization? Why?

What gives a government the right to rule over people?

Are harsh punishments needed to keep people in line?

If the Buddha were alive today, would he still wonder why there is so much suffering in the world?

The arrival of iron technology changed the world in big ways. Is it possible to predict how new technologies will change our world in the future?

Chapter 4

Ancient Greece and Rome: Civilization spreads west

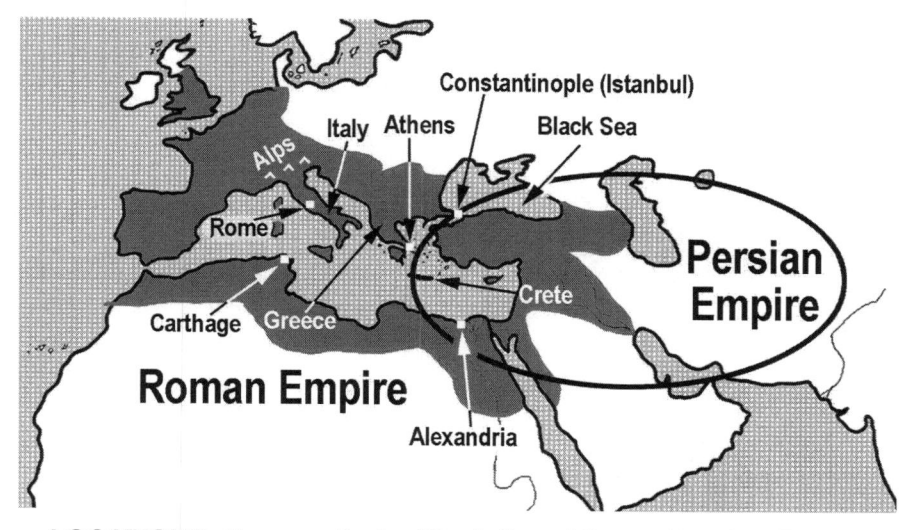

LOCATIONS: Greece, Crete, Black Sea, Athens, Persian Empire (Iran), Alexandria, Italy, Rome, Roman Empire, Carthage, Alps, Constantinople (Istanbul)

Preview

Ancient times began with river valley civilizations, and ancient times ended about 4,000 years later when nomadic raiders brought down great classical civilizations in India, China, and the Mediterranean. This chapter explores the Mediterranean cultures of ancient Greece and Rome, which exerted a great deal of influence on the present-day culture of the Western world.

Classical Greece is considered the birthplace of Western Civilization because it originated many aspects of our culture including literature, philosophy, art, the Olympic games, and democracy. As Greek civilization declined, Roman power grew. Romans learned from the Greeks and made their own contributions to Western Civilization including a legal system and the alphabet we use today.

Greece

The first civilizations to develop in Europe were extensions of the early civilizations of Mesopotamia and Egypt. Europe's earliest major culture was the Minoan civilization of Crete, the largest of the Greek islands. Minoan culture was strongly influenced by Egypt. Minoan civilization is the source of the Greek myth about the hero Theseus, who entered the labyrinth (a maze) and slayed the Minotaur.

Mainland Greece is a mountainous and rocky peninsula with little good farmland, but its long irregular coastline and Greece's numerous islands provided fine harbors. Many Greeks turned to the sea to make a living by fishing and trading. Greeks established colonies and dominated trade in the eastern Mediterranean and in the Black Sea. Greek communities isolated by mountains developed into independent, self-governing city-states that often fought one another. The leading city-states were Sparta with its strong military government and Athens, the present-day capital of Greece. The Greeks had a polytheistic religion; their gods lived on Mount Olympus.

Greece is known for its classical civilization of 500 to 300 BC. Classical Greek culture, particularly that of Athens, is famed for its beautiful arts, architecture, philosophy, theater, Olympic games, and for creating the first democracy. Classical Greece is usually considered the principal source of Western Civilization.

the *Iliad* and the *Odyssey*

Modern people still read literature from ancient Greece, including the *Iliad* and the *Odyssey*, two epic (meaning long and heroic) poems by Homer. The Iliad takes place during the Trojan War, when the Greeks used a large wooden horse with soldiers hidden inside to defeat the defenders of Troy in Asia Minor. The *Odyssey* recounts the adventures of the hero Odysseus, who had to overcome many obstacles during his 10-year voyage home from the war in Troy. These poems are the first literary works of Western Civilization.

The heroes of Greek myths such as the *Iliad* and the *Odyssey* served as models of excellence for the ancient Greeks. In both poems, human brains can be more powerful than physical strength. Homer's Bronze Age poems later inspired a great outpouring of literature during the classical Greek age.

Persian Wars

Centered in present-day Iran, the Persian Empire stretched from the Middle East to India; it was the largest empire the world had yet seen.

Chapter 4 – Ancient Greece and Rome

The Persians tried to add Greece to their empire in the 400s BC, but the Greeks united long enough to defeat them. At the Battle of Marathon, Greeks repelled a larger invading force of Persians, and legend says a Greek soldier ran nearly 26 miles from the battlefield to Athens, where he died after delivering news of the victory. This legend is the basis for the modern marathon foot race.

In fighting ten years later (480 BC), the people of Athens fled to the nearby island of Salamis after the Persians conquered and burned Athens. The Persian king Xerxes had his throne placed on a hill where he could watch his fleet of 700 warships destroy the Greek navy of about 300 ships. Instead, Xerxes watched in horror as the Greeks lured his navy into a narrow strait that prevented many of the Persian ships from joining the battle. The Greeks won the battle, and the Persian Wars soon ended. Because the victory at Salamis preserved Greek culture, some historians have called this "the battle that saved Western Civilization."

Parthenon

A statesman named Pericles became the political leader of Athens after the Persian Wars. Although the wars had ended, Persia remained a military threat, and other Greek city-states paid money to Athens for protection. Pericles used this income to rebuild his burned-out city and to finance the construction of magnificent new buildings including the Parthenon. The Parthenon is a temple built to honor Athena, goddess of wisdom and war and the patron goddess of Athens. The Parthenon is the main building on the Acropolis, a high point in Athens that was the center of Athenian life and a fortress against attack.

Although the Parthenon is now in ruins, it is famed for its beauty and proportion. It may be the most influential building in the history of Western architecture. The Parthenon has served as a model for important buildings in much of the world, including the Lincoln Memorial in the United States. Like all classical Greek temples, the Parthenon was built with closely spaced columns that left little interior space.

democracy

The Greeks established a new kind of society by inventing the polis. The polis was an association of free male citizens who served as the soldiers who defended their city-state from attack, and they managed the government. The polis chose leaders to govern the city-state for a limited period of time, often a year. This approach was quite different from other ancient societies in which government was headed by a king, and the people were separated by class into a small group of the rich and a large group of the poor.

The democratic principles developed in the polis reached their greatest extent during the rule of Pericles in Athens, where every citizen was expected to participate in government. Democracy is a form of government in which power lies with the people who, may exercise that power *directly* as they did in ancient Athens, where all citizens could vote on new laws. Or power may be exercised *indirectly* through elected representatives as we do in the United States. Most of the Greek city-states did not have democratic governments, and even in Athens, citizens were a minority of the population because women, slaves, and foreign-born persons did not qualify as citizens.

humanism

The ancient Greeks considered human beings to be the center of existence. Unlike other ancient cultures that were deeply concerned with religion, gods, and the afterlife, the philosophy and arts of classical Greece were more concerned with the value of human beings on earth. This emphasis on humans can be seen in Greek art that portrayed the human body realistically. Art of the classical Greek period was much more realistic than the stiff, formal art of earlier eras such as the art of ancient Egypt and early Greece.

Greeks strived for excellence in the way they conducted their daily lives. They believed that reason was the true source of knowledge and that a wise person was the best person; reason, not emotion, should rule our lives. This concern with human life, and the effort to improve humanity through reason, is called humanism. Greek humanism emphasized order in daily life, nothing in excess, a balance between extremes known as "The Golden Mean." In school, for example, both the body and the mind were trained. Over two thousand years later, Greek humanism would help shape the Renaissance and the Enlightenment in Europe.

Socrates (SOCK-ruh-tees)

Talented artists and thinkers were drawn to Athens during the Age of Pericles. One of the best known was the philosopher Socrates. He was famed for saying, "The unexamined life is not worth living." Socrates encouraged his students to question accepted wisdom including government policies.

But the golden age of Athens came to end as Athens went to war with Sparta. Early in the fighting, a plague of typhoid fever killed a third of the residents of Athens, including Pericles. After 27 years of warfare, Athens was defeated and went into decline. Socrates was condemned to death by the citizens of Athens for neglecting the gods and corrupting the morals of the young. Many historians believe, however, that Socrates was made a scapegoat for the decline of Athens after it was defeated by Sparta.

Socrates did not leave behind written works; his philosophy was carried forward by his student, Plato. Plato was deeply troubled by the death of his friend Socrates. It caused him to question democracy; Plato warned that clever leaders could easily manipulate citizens who knew little about the important issues of the day. Plato established a school called The Academy, the first real university. His most famous student was the philosopher Aristotle, whose ideas would dominate Western scientific thought for centuries to come.

Hellenistic Civilization

Despite the decline of Athens, Greece would again take the center stage of history with the conquests of Alexander the Great, a young man from the mountainous northern region of Greece called Macedonia. Alexander's tutor was the philosopher Aristotle, and his father was Philip of Macedon, who succeeded in conquering all of Greece in 338 BC, ending the independence of the Greek city-states. After his father died, Alexander took control of Greece at the age of 20, but Alexander wanted more.

Alexander succeeded in conquering Egypt and much of the ancient world, extending his empire all the way to India. In the process, he defeated Greece's old enemy, the Persian Empire. Alexander never lost a battle, but he became sick with fever and died at the age of 32. His empire fell apart and was divided among his top generals.

After his death, a new culture emerged known as Hellenistic civilization, a blend of Greek, Persian, Egyptian, and Indian influences that would flourish for centuries. One of the cities founded by Alexander, Alexandria, Egypt, had a great library that was the center of learning for the Hellenistic world.

Roman Empire

Rome, the capital of present-day Italy, was also the capital of the ancient Roman Empire. The Romans were a practical and hardworking people, and Rome's sturdy farmers made good soldiers. Rome was only a small town on the Tiber River when Athens was at the height of its glory, but Rome grew to become a strong city-state around the time of Alexander the Great.

The Romans adopted Hellenistic culture; their gods, arts, and architecture resembled those of the Greeks. At first, kings ruled Rome, and then about 500 BC, the Roman Republic was established with a law-making body called the Senate. (A republic is similar to a democracy, but the term may imply representative government or greater personal rights.)

Every year the Senate chose two of its members to serve as co-rulers, or consuls. For a time, Rome had a form of democracy, although wealthy upper-class families held most of the political power. Later, during a time of trouble in the republic, Julius Caesar seized control of the government. His successors took the title of emperor.

At its height, the Roman Empire completely encircled the Mediterranean Sea, extending from the Middle East to the British Isles. Rome's central location in the Mediterranean made it an ideal location for building a large Mediterranean empire and international trading network. It was said, "All roads lead to Rome." The empire had a strong central government that produced massive public works including paved roads, government buildings, baths, sports arenas, and aqueducts (water transport structures). As the years passed, the Roman Empire weakened, was divided into two parts, and eventually it fell to nomadic invaders.

Carthage

Carthage was an ancient city on the coast of North Africa, and a powerful rival of Rome. From 264-146 BC, Carthage and the Roman Republic fought three Punic Wars. During the second war, a general from Carthage named Hannibal led a huge army supported by war elephants from Spain through the Alps into Italy, a troop movement considered one of the greatest in history. Hannibal could not be stopped, and he was threatening Rome when Roman armies attacked Carthage, forcing Hannibal to return to protect his homeland. Hannibal later poisoned himself rather than become a prisoner of the Romans.

In the third and final Punic War, Roman armies burned Carthage to the ground, and the people of Carthage became Roman slaves. As in ancient Greece, much of Rome's work was done by slave labor. With Carthage defeated, Rome was free to expand into new territories including Spain, Greece, and Egypt.

Julius Caesar

Turmoil came to the Roman Republic following the Punic Wars. Small farmers could not compete with cheaper agricultural products and slave labor imported from the conquered territories. Farmers lost their land to rich landowners and drifted to the cities. Mobs of poor people rioted in the streets of Rome demanding more power. Civil war broke out when a successful general, Julius Caesar, moved his army out of Gaul (present-day France) and marched toward Rome. Caesar won the civil war, and he had the Senate declare him dictator for life in 48 BC, ending the Roman Republic that had existed for over 400 years.

Caesar was assassinated on the Ides of March (March 15) in 44 BC by his friend Brutus and other senators opposed to Caesar's dictatorship. Brutus and his fellow assassins wanted Rome to remain a republic. It didn't. While some people believed Caesar was an arrogant tyrant, others gave him credit for restoring order at a time when Rome's republican government was no longer functioning effectively.

Pax Romana

During a trip to Egypt, Caesar fell in love with Cleopatra, the young queen of Egypt, and he brought her with him to Rome. After Caesar's death, Cleopatra returned to Egypt, and civil war broke out again in Rome between Caesar's supporters and his killers. Caesar's friends won the struggle, and two of them took control of the empire, Octavian in the west and Antony in the east. When Antony traveled to Egypt, he too fell in love with Cleopatra even though he was married to Octavian's sister. In Rome, Octavian declared war on Antony and Cleopatra, and he eventually defeated their combined military forces. To avoid being captured, Antony and Cleopatra committed suicide. While alive, Cleopatra tried to keep Egypt great. After her death, Egypt became a province of the Roman Empire, ending the 3,000-year reign of the pharaohs.

Octavian became sole ruler of Rome and took the name Augustus. Considered a political genius by many, Augustus proclaimed himself Rome's first emperor, and he was worshipped as a god. He quietly stripped the Senate of its power, turning Rome into an empire disguised as a republic. Nonetheless, the reign of Augustus ended nearly a century of political strife in the Roman world, and it was the beginning of a 200-year period of peace and prosperity called Pax Romana, Latin for the "Roman Peace."

Roman law

Rome's empire grew to its largest size during the Pax Romana. One way Roman emperors controlled their vast empire was through a uniform system of laws that was enforced from one end of the Roman world to the other. Judges were required to weigh evidence fairly, and accused persons were considered innocent until proven guilty. The courts enforced legal contracts. These principles were later adopted in legal systems of other nations including the United States. Roman law is one of the greatest legacies of the empire.

The empire was also held together by a well-trained army, by communications over an extensive road system, and by the Latin language.

The Latin alphabet was derived from an earlier writing system created by sea traders from Phoenicia at the eastern end of the Mediterranean Sea. From their travels, Phoenicians learned about Sumerian cuneiform and Egyptian hieroglyphics, writing systems that used hundreds of symbols to represent words or syllables.

The Phoenicians had a better idea; they created just 22 symbols to represent spoken sounds. We call these symbols letters. Because the Phoenician Alphabet was simpler and more precise than picture writing, it spread to other cultures. It was adopted by the Greeks, who added vowels, and by the Romans, who modified the letters to become the alphabet we use today.

arch

An arch is a curved opening that spans a doorway, window, or other space. The arch could span much greater distances than the column-and-beam architecture of the Egyptians and Greeks. Arches built side-by-side created aqueducts; arches placed in front of one another formed large "vaulted" ceilings, and arches arranged in a circular pattern created domes. The arch was adopted on a large scale by the Romans, who also developed the use of concrete as a construction material. The arch and concrete made it possible to construct public buildings with large interior spaces that could be used for practical purposes, not just as temples.

One of the most impressive of these buildings is the Colosseum, a great arena of ancient Rome that seated 50,000 spectators. Bloody and deadly contests were staged in the Colosseum for the entertainment of Roman citizens. Although the Colosseum is now in ruins, it remains a monument to Roman engineering, and it is the symbol of the present-day city of Rome. The Colosseum also stands as a monument to human cruelty that symbolizes the decadence, or moral decay, of the later years of the Roman Empire.

Constantine the Great

By the fourth century AD, the Roman Empire was in confusion; it was running short of money and facing increasing pressure from raiders pushing in from the borders. In one 50-year period, 26 emperors reigned, and only one of them died of natural causes. At about this time a strong general named Constantine took control of the empire and tried to stop its decline. He is remembered as Constantine the Great.

Although Christianity had long been outlawed in the empire, Constantine legalized Christianity, and he ended the blood sports in the Colosseum. He also established Constantinople as the capital of the stronger eastern part of the Roman Empire, while Rome remained capital of the weakened western part of the empire.

Constantine ruled over both parts of the empire from Constantinople on the Bosporus Strait that connects the Black Sea to the Mediterranean. Constantinople was a prosperous crossroads of trade routes where Europe meets Asia. Today, Constantinople is called Istanbul, and it is Turkey's largest city.

Fall of Rome

The fall of Rome was a slow-motion process that took centuries to unfold. Despite the best efforts of Constantine, the Roman Empire continued to decline after his death, as nomadic warriors stepped up their attacks. These nomads included the Huns, who swept down from the Eurasian steppes, pushing other nomadic tribes like the Goths and the Vandals ahead of them. Many nomads were simply seeking a better life inside the empire. But the Romans considered these nomadic peoples to be culturally inferior and called them barbarians. Near the end, the Roman Empire was in chaos, hiring barbarians to fight other barbarians.

The last emperor in the west was defeated in 476 AD, the date usually given as the Fall of Rome. It should be remembered, however, that the eastern portion of the Roman Empire lived on for another thousand years as the Byzantine Empire. Historians have long debated the causes of the Fall of Rome. Factors included a terrible plague, the decline of agriculture, heavy taxes, and a decadent upper class devoted to luxury and greed.

Some questions to consider:

Are the actions of people and of nations ruled more by reason or by emotion?

Are there similarities between the Chinese idea of Yin Yang and the Greek idea of the Golden Mean?

Is democracy fragile like an egg or strong like a rock?

Was Plato right to be worried that clever leaders can manipulate citizens in a democracy?

Chapter 5

Early Middle Ages: 500 to 1000 AD

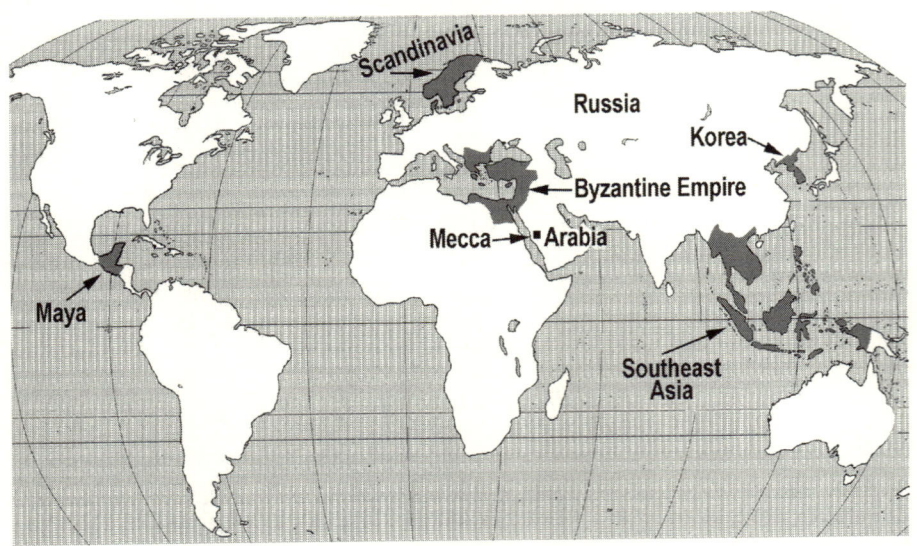

LOCATIONS: Byzantine Empire, Scandinavia, Russia, Southeast Asia, Korea, Maya, Arabia, Mecca

Preview

When the great classical civilizations of India, China, and the Mediterranean fell to nomadic invaders around 500 AD, ancient times ended, and the middle ages* began: a thousand-year-long period between ancient times and modern times.

Although major civilizations had fallen, civilizations still flourished in the eastern half of the old Roman Empire and in America. Civilization would soon return to China, and a powerful new Islamic civilization was about to be born in the Middle East.

---

*The term *middle ages* is not capitalized here because the term is not being used to identify a specific period of European history but to designate a period of world history much as the terms *ancient times* and *modern times* are used.

46

the classical period

The classical period came at the end of ancient times. Ancient times began with the early river valley civilizations starting about 3500 BC and ended with the fall of classical civilizations around 500 AD. When people in the West speak of the classical period, they usually mean ancient Greece and Rome. But in a larger sense, a classical period is when any civilization undergoes advancement in several fields such as religion, government, or the arts. It's a time when a culture develops features that help to define it far into the future.

The great classical civilizations of India, China, and the Mediterranean created larger empires than had existed before. They all suffered from internal weaknesses before falling to Hun invasions by about 500 AD, marking the end of ancient times. Still, each civilization had its own distinctive character. The Mauryan and Gupta dynasties gave India religious philosophies that focused on union with a universal spiritual force and de-emphasized the concerns of this life. The Qin and Han dynasties left China with a tradition of strong central governments headed by powerful rulers and a Confucian philosophy that promoted order, respect, and learning. Greece and Rome gave Western Civilization a humanistic philosophy concerned with improving life through reason, along with traditions of citizen involvement in government and rule by law.

the middle ages

Historians disagree about the best way to classify eras of history, but many people use the term *middle ages* to identify the period between ancient times and modern times, a thousand years from approximately 500 AD to 1500 AD. Although civilization was in decline at the beginning of this period, a powerful new Islamic civilization was about to arise in the Middle East, and older civilizations would eventually revive. During the middle ages, international trade would grow, helping to spread civilization and major religions from core civilizations to outlying regions including sub-Saharan Africa, Japan, and Russia.

The first few centuries of the middle ages in Europe are often called the Dark Ages because civilization had collapsed after the Fall of Rome, and Europe was torn by widespread fighting among barbarian tribes. We shall begin our journey through the middle ages in Europe, where civilization had fallen the farthest.

Germanic tribes

Although the Romans called them barbarians, German-speaking nomads defeated the Romans because the empire had grown weak, and it could no longer defend its vast borders. But the Germanic tribes were illiterate (could not read and write), and warriors were loyal only to their local chiefs, which made the development of nations or empires impossible. This was a time of much warfare between competing tribes and bands; the populations of cities declined as people fled to the countryside to escape the fighting.

The loss of writing, cities, and government organization meant that civilization had largely ended in Western Europe. As time went on, barbarian chiefs would become nobles and kings, and these German-speaking tribes would evolve into the powerful kingdoms that ruled Europe later during the middle ages.

Christianity

Christianity took hold in the Roman Empire as the empire was falling apart. It was based on the Old Testament of the Bible and the teachings of Jesus, a Jewish holy man born in the Middle East during the reign of Augustus Caesar. Jesus encouraged his followers to be kind to others and to reject violence. Jewish leaders disagreed with some of Jesus's teachings and had him placed on trial. He was executed by Roman officials.

Later, the Roman Empire adopted Christianity as its official religion, which spread Christianity over a large area and made Christianity a major world religion. Today it is the world's largest religion.

The Roman Catholic Church was one institution from Roman times that did not break down. During the Dark Ages, Latin-educated Catholics kept the flame of learning alive in Western Europe. Even the Germanic tribes converted to Christianity by about 600 AD. Over time, the bishop of Rome came to be accepted as the leader of the Catholic Church, the pope.

Christianity, like other major religions of the time, came to dominate art, architecture, and thinking in the lands where it was adopted. Christianity was so central to life during the middle ages in Europe that Western Europe was called Christendom.

Charlemagne

We begin to see civilization returning to Europe with the reign of Charlemagne, the Christian king of a Germanic people called the Franks. The Franks gave France its name. Charlemagne established a large empire in western and central Europe. After his armies defended the pope, the pope crowned Charlemagne as the new Roman emperor on Christmas day in the year 800. This attempt to revive the western Roman Empire didn't last long. When Charlemagne died, his empire was divided among his three sons. Two of these kingdoms formed the general outlines of today's Germany and France.

In addition to his success as a warrior, Charlemagne is remembered for his encouragement of learning: he needed reading and writing to manage a large empire. Charlemagne established schools and surrounded himself with scholars. He encouraged monks in monasteries to copy literature from the ancient Greeks and Romans; without this work, much of what we know about the classical world would have been lost forever.

Monasteries were Catholic religious communities where monks raised their own food, operated schools and libraries, and copied books. Catholic nuns had similar institutions called convents, which were one place in Europe where women could receive an education and live free of male control.

Vikings

Vikings were fierce warriors, traders, and raiders from Scandinavia, present-day Norway, Sweden, and Denmark. During the 800s and 900s, Vikings terrorized much of coastal Europe and traveled far inland by river to loot, destroy, and slaughter. They fought the Franks among others, and they conquered Normandy (land of the Northmen) in northern France, where they settled down and converted to Christianity.

Vikings traveled the stormy North Atlantic in excellent ships that could also navigate shallow rivers. The Vikings brought the adventurous spirit of ocean exploration to Europe. A Viking named Leif Erickson was probably the first European explorer to discover North America, but little resulted from his visit.

feudalism

Farming villages in Europe needed defense against waves of nasty invaders like the Vikings. The solution was mounted warriors called knights who could respond quickly to an attack. The invention of the stirrup gave knights a steady platform from which to fight while wearing heavy metal armor and using heavy weapons. Local lords (the nobility) hired knights to protect villagers because the villagers' farms provided the lord's income. The farmers, called serfs, were not slaves but were poor and had few rights.

The lord, in turn, owed military service to the king who granted the lord his land. In this way, the king ruled through local lords who controlled smaller territories within the kingdom.

This kind of military and social system is called feudalism. Under feudalism, people owed loyalty and service to those above, while those above owed protection to those below. Feudalism was a middle stage in the development of government between rule by tribes and rule by large nations with centralized governments that would come later.

Conditions in Western Europe had gradually improved since the Dark Ages. The feudal system offered people some protection, and the church provided cultural unity and the hope of a better life in heaven. But Christendom was divided among many competing kingdoms, and commercial activity was weak. In the early middle ages, Europe was still a backward society compared to the great civilizations of Eurasia.

Byzantine Empire

One of the world's great civilizations was next door to Europe in the eastern part of the Roman Empire, the part that did not fall to barbarians. The eastern Roman Empire survived for another thousand years under a new name, the Byzantine Empire with its capital at Constantinople. The size of the empire fluctuated over the centuries, but it generally included Greece and Asia Minor. Byzantine culture extended into Russia.

Byzantine emperors served as head of both the Christian Church and the state. Greek replaced Latin as the official language. Eventually the Christian Church split into eastern and western branches, with Latin-speaking Roman Catholics in Western Europe and Greek-speaking Orthodox Christians in the East.

Byzantine emperors promoted a style of art that featured beautiful mosaics. The best-known example of Byzantine architecture is the church of Saint Sophia constructed by Emperor Justinian in Constantinople. Built as the largest Christian Church in the world, it became the model for later Eastern Orthodox Churches.

Justinian also brought together all of the laws of the Roman Empire into a single legal code that became the basis for modern legal systems in Europe. Rules and customs in the Byzantine court became so complex that the term *byzantine* is now used to indicate any set of complicated laws or procedures.

Russia

Viking traders moved into western Russia and developed river trade routes that reached south to Constantinople. Furs from Scandinavia were traded for luxury products from the Byzantine Empire. Many Russians visited Constantinople, and missionaries traveled to Russia spreading the Eastern Orthodox religion. One of Russia's early rulers, a Viking descendent named Vladimir I, married the sister of a Byzantine emperor, and he accepted Orthodox Christianity for his people. His choice of Christianity might have been influenced by Islam's ban on alcohol. He reportedly said, "Drinking is the joy of the Russes."

Russia's culture, including its art and architecture, began to resemble Byzantine culture. The Russian alphabet is derived from the Greek alphabet, and Orthodox Christianity is the main religion in Russia today.

Tang Dynasty (TONG)

In China, nearly four centuries of disorder followed the fall of the Han Dynasty in 220 AD. During this long period of unrest, Buddhism gained strength in China. China finally became united again under a new emperor in the early middle ages, and shortly thereafter the Tang Dynasty took control of China and returned China to greatness. Under the Tang, the ideals of Confucius were revived; art and music flourished, and gunpowder and printing were invented. The Chinese first printed by carving words and pictures into blocks of wood, which were pressed against paper. Later the Chinese invented movable type, with each character made from a single piece of hardened clay.

Tang emperors tried to improve agriculture by reducing large estates held by aristocrats and giving land to the peasants (poor and uneducated farmers). During the Tang period, China's economy was enriched by the new Grand Canal dug between the Yellow and the Yangtze Rivers. Canal boats now linked the political center of north China with the prosperous rice-producing Yangtze River basin in the south. Safe and inexpensive canal transportation brought more rice, precious goods, and taxes to northern China. The Tang dynasty lasted for three hundred years, from 618 to 907 AD. It weakened and was replaced by the Song Dynasty that continued China's economic and cultural development for another three hundred years.

Southeast Asia

One of the most important events of the middle ages was the spread of rice farming in Asia. After a new and more productive variety of rice became available, large tracts of swampland and forest were converted to rice paddies. In China, population doubled between the 700s and 1100s. This new type of rice originated in Southeast Asia and reached China and India over ocean trade routes. These same routes brought manufactured goods such as scissors and cooking pots to Southeast Asia.

Southeast Asia is a region comprising two parts: the southeast corner of the Asian mainland and a large archipelago (chain of islands) between the Asian mainland and Australia. It includes the modern mainland countries of Vietnam and Thailand, and the island nations of Indonesia and the Philippines.

Sailors of Southeast Asia were among the world's most daring. During ancient times, they discovered how to ride the monsoons, seasonal winds that blow toward the continent of Asia during the warm months and away from the mainland during the cold months. These sailors opened the southern ocean trade routes that connected the Indian trading network with the China trade network. By the early middle ages, they were sailing two-thirds of the way around the earth from Africa to islands in the South Pacific.

Korea and Japan

As rice cultivation spread from the central civilizations of Asia, new societies began to develop in outlying regions. Rice growing became important in Korea about 100 AD, and rice took hold in Japan over a century later. Other imports from China and India soon followed. Buddhist monks brought reading, writing, and their religion first to Korea and then to Japan. Both countries adopted Chinese architectural styles. Rulers in Korea and Japan tried to organize central governments based on the Chinese model.

Korea, a peninsula attached to the Chinese mainland, was strongly influenced by China. Japan, an archipelago separated from China by 500 miles of ocean, was somewhat less affected by Chinese culture. Both societies managed to retain distinct cultures by blending Chinese influences with their own traditions.

As was generally true in civilized societies during the middle ages, women in Japan had fewer rights than men. Nonetheless, upper-class women studied art and music, and they learned how to read and write. Japanese women produced some of finest literature of the age including *The Tale of Genji* about life in the royal court. *The Tale of Genji* is believed to be the first novel written in any language.

the Maya

Humans came late to the Western Hemisphere, and civilization started later here too. Native Americans were isolated from advancements in Eurasia, so they had to invent agriculture and civilization on their own. Agriculture appeared in Mexico and South America about 5,000 years after it began in the Middle East.

The first civilization of the Americas was probably the Olmec culture of southern Mexico (1200 BC to 400 BC). The Olmecs raised corn, beans, and squash, and are known for their sculptures of giant stone heads.

The Maya Civilization arose centuries later just east of Olmec lands. Maya city-states flourished between 300 and 900 AD in the Yucatan peninsula of Mexico and northern Central America.

The Maya improved on the achievements of the Olmecs to create the most advanced native civilization of the Americas. They used hieroglyphics to write on stone and in books made of bark paper. They had a zero-based numbering system before the Europeans did. They created fine arts, a calendar of 365¼ days, and impressive pyramid-shaped temples in large cities. The Maya also practiced human sacrifice and apparently played a ball game that ended in death. Perhaps the Maya were too successful; it appears that they overpopulated their land, depleting it of natural resources, which contributed to their decline.

Muhammad

One of the biggest historical events of the middle ages came out of the harsh deserts of the Arabian peninsula: the birth of Muhammad and his religion of Islam. Arabia was a land of camel caravans, a few trading cities, and fierce desert nomads called Bedouins. Bedouin tribes worshiped local gods and fought one another. Muhammad was born in the city of Mecca, where he became a successful caravan trader and merchant. From his travels, Muhammad learned of Judaism and Christianity, religions with only one God.

Although Muhammad was prosperous and respected, he wanted more than a life devoted to material wealth. He was troubled by inequality between rich merchants and poor nomads. Muhammad would often go off by himself to think and meditate. One day he saw a vision of the angel Gabriel, who told him to "recite" messages from God. Muhammad began to teach these messages, and eventually they were written in a holy book called the Qur'an. Muhammad's teachings led to conflicts with the rulers of Mecca, who threatened his life. In 622 AD, he fled to the nearby town of Medina, where his religious teachings and wise advice gained him many followers

Muhammad also proved to be an effective military leader when his followers battled forces from Mecca. In 630 AD, Muhammad with thousands of followers returned to Mecca in victory. Muhammad died just two years later, but he is revered as the chief prophet or messenger of Islam.

Islam

Worshipers of Islam are called Muslims, their houses of worship are mosques, and their God is Allah. Today Islam is the world's second-largest religion. Most Muslims live in a geographic band that stretches from Morocco in west Africa to the islands of Southeast Asia. Muslims believe Allah is the same God worshiped by Jews and Christians; Muhammad said Islam is a refinement of these two earlier religions.

Rather than relying on priests, Muslims have a direct relationship with God (although Muslims have worship leaders called imams). Muslims are expected to help the poor and sick and to be kind and generous to those of lower rank. Muslims face Mecca five times a day to pray, and they are encouraged to go on a pilgrimage (religious journey) to Mecca.

Muhammad taught that all men and women are equal before God; women in early Muslim societies had more rights than women in many other cultures of the time. Muslim scholars developed the Shari'a (Shuh-REE-uh), a legal and moral code based on Islamic teachings that applied to government, business, and personal dealings. Under Shari'a law, there was no separation between religion and government.

Arab conquests

Islam gave Arabia's Bedouin tribes one God to worship, and it promoted equality among believers. The tribes experienced a unity they had never known before. Rather than fighting each other, they went on a spree of foreign conquest aided by fast Arabian horses and camels well suited to desert warfare. These were wars of territorial conquest, not holy wars; Arabs did not attempt to spread Islam to lands they conquered.

Arabs subdued Persia to their east, parts of the Byzantine Empire to the north, and Egypt to the west. Then they took a breather to quarrel over who was the rightful heir to Muhammad.

After splitting into two sects, the Sunni and Shi'a, the Arabs resumed their conquests in northern India, North Africa, and Spain. But when they tried to expand farther into Christian Europe, they were stopped by the Franks in the west and by the Byzantine Empire in the east. In just a hundred years, Arabs created the largest empire since Rome.

Chapter 5 – Early Middle Ages: 500 to 1000 AD

Some questions to consider:

Why might it be difficult to create a large empire without officials who can read and write?

Based on the historical evidence you have seen, do all major cultures, empires, and civilizations follow a general pattern of growth, flowering, and decline?

Will the United States eventually decline? Has its decline already begun?

Consider the Qin Dynasty in China, Maya civilization in America, and the Roman Empire in Europe. Based on this evidence, would it be reasonable to conclude that empires and civilizations oftentimes contribute to their own downfall?

Chapter 6

Late Middle Ages: 1000 to 1500

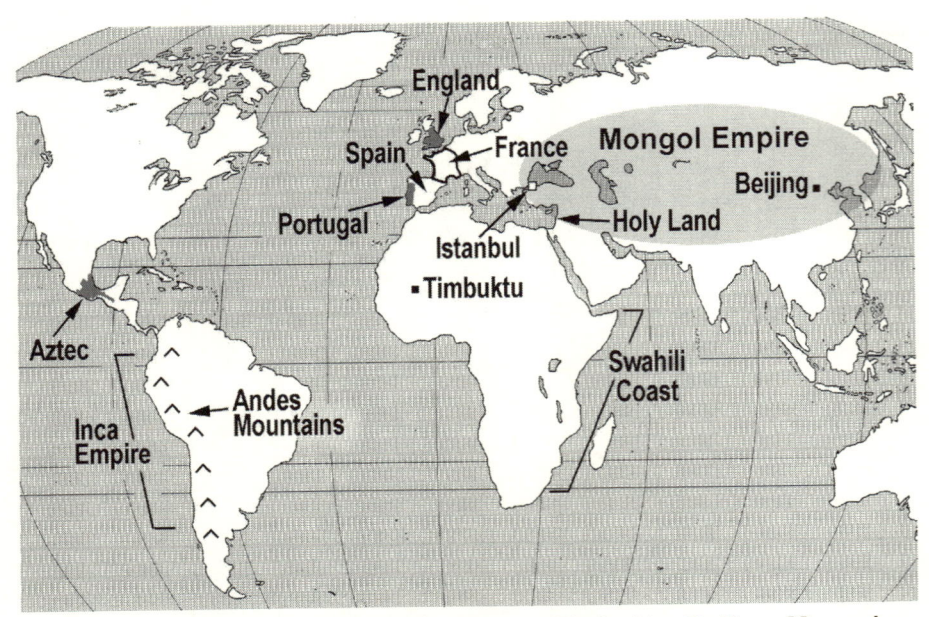

LOCATIONS: Holy Land, Swahili Coast, Timbuktu, Beijing, Mongol Empire, Istanbul, France, England, Andes Mountains, Aztec, Inca, Spain, Portugal

Preview

In this chapter, we move from the first half of the middle ages into the second half, when Islam will spread to new lands in Asia and Africa, and terrifying Mongol raiders will sweep out of the Asian steppes to create the greatest land empire in world history.

After sending huge treasure ships to the far reaches of the known world, China will pull back from ocean exploration, giving Europeans the opportunity to make the great voyages of discovery that will finally unite the Eastern and Western Hemispheres and change the world—voyages that mark the end of the middle ages and the beginning of "modern times."

Abbasid Empire (uh-BA-suhd)

The Arab world came under control of the Abbasid Dynasty in 750 AD. The great wave of Arabic conquest was over, and people of many lands were choosing to adopt Islam as their religion. Muslim traders, sailors, and preachers carried Islam to new territories in Central Asia, sub-Saharan Africa, and Southeast Asia. People converted to Islam because it promised a close relationship with God and equality among believers, and Muslims enjoyed the benefits of membership in a large and prosperous society.

Abbasid rulers were tolerant of different peoples and open to new ideas. Jews, Christians, Hindus, and Buddhists enjoyed freedom of religion in Muslim lands. Muslims learned from the cultures they encountered. They preserved the works of Aristotle and other classical Greek writers. They adopted the zero-based numbering system of India. They acquired the compass and papermaking from China. And they developed one of the most creative societies of all time. Islamic literature, art, and architecture flowered. Islamic civilization surpassed all others in science and technology and in size.

But the very size of the Abbasid Empire made it difficult to govern. At the same time the Islamic world was reaching new heights of achievement, Abbasid rulers were losing control of their empire to non-Arabs. As the empire weakened, it broke into a number of competing Islamic kingdoms and then fell to nomadic invaders.

the Swahili Coast

It was during the Abbasid Dynasty that Muslim traders brought sub-Saharan Africa into closer contact with the rest of the world and spread the religion of Islam in the process. As Muslim merchants developed trade links with cities in East and West Africa, African rulers in these trade centers often converted to Islam.

One trade center was on the east coast of Africa, where the Swahili language was spoken. A string of prosperous Swahili Coast cities connected East Africa to the southern ocean trading network. These ports traded gold, ivory, and slaves from Africa for cotton from India, silk from Persia, and porcelain from China.

Empire of Mali

Islam came to West Africa with camel caravans crossing the Sahara Desert from North Africa. Camels could go no farther south than a band of savanna lying on the southern edge of the desert because camels sickened in wetter climates to the south.

Trading cities such as Timbuktu grew and prospered where caravans stopped and exchanged salt and other goods from the north for gold from sub-Saharan Africa.

Several large states developed around these trading cities in the "hump" of West Africa. One was the Empire of Mali, which thrived during the 1200s and 1300s. A Mali ruler, Mansa Musa, went on a pilgrimage to Mecca in 1324 and distributed so much gold on his journey that the value of gold dropped in Egypt.

Although Islam came to African trade centers, much of the interior of Africa was untouched by Muslim culture. People there continued to follow traditional religions, and many lived in stateless societies without formal rulers. In stateless societies, the community or a council of families made decisions.

Crusades

While the Abbasid Dynasty was struggling to maintain control over its weakening empire, it faced a new threat from Europe. Roman Catholic popes encouraged Christian kings and knights to undertake military expeditions, or Crusades, to capture the Holy Land from the Muslims. The Holy Land is a region at the eastern end of the Mediterranean Sea where Jesus lived; it is also holy to Jews and Muslims. Christian crusaders conquered much of the Holy Land, taking Jerusalem in 1099, but they were unable to hold it and were driven out by 1291. These Christian invasions are still recalled with bitterness by some Muslims.

Still, the Crusades probably had greater impact on Europe than on the Holy Land. Europeans now had firsthand knowledge of just how backward Europe seemed in comparison to the more advanced Islamic culture. This realization probably pushed Europeans to develop more rapidly to catch up with the rival Muslims. Europeans acquired important technologies from the Muslim world including the "Arabic" numbering system (from India), the compass (from China), and the astrolabe, an Arabic instrument for measuring latitude. These inventions would make it possible for European ships to sail far out to sea.

Mongols

The Abbasid Empire fell when Mongol invaders conquered the capital of Baghdad in 1258 and massacred some 800,000 Muslims including the caliph (emperor). The Mongols were nomadic tribesmen and superb mounted warriors from central Asia who swept east toward China and west toward Europe under the brilliant but ruthless leadership of Genghis Khan and his successors. Mongols created the largest land empire in world history.

The Mongol conquests stopped just short of Western Europe when a Mongol leader died, and generals returned home to choose a new khan. Genghis Khan's grandson, Kublai Khan, completed the conquest of China. He made himself emperor of China and established the present-day capital of Beijing.

The Mongols left their mark. It took time for many regions to recover from Mongol destruction. The Mongol defeat of the Abbasid Dynasty left the Muslim world fragmented, and Mongol control slowed the development of Russia. But a Mongol law code established order across the vast Mongol Empire, ushering in a period of peace and increased trade between East and West over the old Silk Roads.

These trade routes also transported the fleas that carried the Black Death (bubonic plague) from China to the Middle East and to Europe, where it killed half the people of some areas. The Mongols were warriors, not administrators, and they did not develop the government institutions necessary to maintain an empire. Mongol unity withered in the late 1300s, and eventually the Mongols were absorbed into the cultures they had conquered.

Marco Polo

The Mongol invasions marked nearly the last time in history that nomadic raiders would threaten civilization. Settled societies, with superior military organization and firearms, eventually gained the upper hand against nomads. Because Western Europe was spared from Mongol attacks, Europe benefited in several ways from the Mongol conquests. The Mongol victories weakened Europe's Muslim rivals, and when the Mongols reestablished dependable trade along the Silk Road, Europeans acquired new knowledge and technology from the East, including gunpowder weapons.

In Europe, Venice, Italy grew wealthy as the main trading crossroads between East and West. In 1271, a teenager from Venice named Marco Polo left on a trading trip to China with his father and uncle. They visited the court of Kublai Khan, who gave bright young Marco a job as ambassador to outlying regions of China.

Marco returned to Italy 24 years later and was serving as captain of a Venetian warship when he was captured and sent to prison in Genoa, Italy. There he wrote what is probably the most influential travel book of all time, *The Travels of Marco Polo*. The book gave Europeans their first real knowledge of China, and about two centuries later it inspired another Italian, Christopher Columbus of Genoa, to set sail for Asia.

samurai

Although Kublai Khan ruled China, he failed to conquer Japan. In 1281, he sent a fleet of over 4,000 ships and 150,000 warriors against Japan. Japan appeared to be doomed until two days of typhoon winds destroyed much of the Chinese force. The Japanese called the storm *kamikaze*, or "divine wind."

At this time, warlords ruled Japan, and Japan had a feudal system very similar to the system in Europe. Poor farmers were bound to a landowning lord, and the lord protected his holdings with mounted professional warriors called samurai. Some members of the samurai class became rulers in their own right.

the voyages of Zheng He
(JUNG HUH, sometimes spelled Cheng Ho)

The Chinese resented being ruled by Mongol outsiders. After the death of Kublai Khan, a revolt drove the Mongols from China and established the Ming Dynasty, which lasted nearly 300 years. The Ming are known for their fine blue and white porcelain (or china) that was exported to much of the world. The Ming built the Forbidden City in Beijing as a new home for the emperor with beautiful palaces and gardens.

In the early 1400s, Ming emperors sent Chinese admiral Zheng He—a Muslim and a eunuch—on seven great overseas voyages to demonstrate Chinese power and to collect treasure. On his first expedition, Zheng He commanded a fleet of 62 ships and 28,000 men. Some of his treasure ships were over 400 feet long, many times the size of the ships later used by Columbus. These expeditions traveled as far as Arabia and east Africa, extending Chinese influence over much of the civilized world.

But Ming court advisers began to argue that China could learn nothing from foreign "barbarians," and China's money would be better spent closer to home improving defenses against Mongols and other nomads. The ocean expeditions stopped, and China's fleet went into decline. China's withdrawal from ocean exploration opened the door for the less-advanced civilization in Western Europe to explore and eventually dominate the world's oceans.

Ottoman Empire

Following the Mongol disruptions, three new Islamic empires emerged to replace the fallen Abbasid Dynasty. They were the Ottoman Empire in the eastern Mediterranean, the Safavid Empire in Persia, and the Mughal Empire of India. (A Mughal ruler built the famed Taj Mahal.) Of these three empires, the Ottoman Empire was the largest, and it lasted longest.

The Ottomans were a branch of Turkish nomads from central Asia who fled west to escape the Mongols. They settled in Asia Minor and eventually extended their rule to Christian lands in southern Europe and to Muslim lands in the Middle East. The Ottoman Turks conquered the last remaining piece of the old Byzantine Empire in 1453, when they used early cannons to destroy the walls of Constantinople. They made the city their capital and renamed it Istanbul.

The Ottoman Turks were Sunni Muslims. Their neighbors in the Safavid Empire were Shi'a Muslims. The two empires battled for dominance, a struggle intensified by their religious differences. Today Shi'a Muslims remain concentrated in the vicinity of Persia, now Iran and Iraq, while Sunnis are a majority elsewhere. Distracted by conflicts with their rivals and by internal problems, the three Islamic empires paid little attention to the growing commercial and technological strength of the kingdoms in Europe.

guilds

In Europe of the late middle ages, improvements in agricultural technology led to bigger populations and the growth of cities. Townspeople gradually won the right from their local lords to run their own city governments. Trade grew, and cities became important centers of manufacturing and commerce.

Many of the goods traded in Europe were produced by self-employed craftspeople who formed organizations called guilds to regulate the price and quality of their products such as shoes or metalwork. Guilds were the forerunners of today's labor unions. Guilds also served as civic organizations that helped to run the towns. Some women began taking up trades like hat making or weaving that gave them greater financial independence. Merchants and craftspeople were becoming a new class in European society, a middle class between the peasants and the nobility (lords and kings).

Hundred Years' War

It might be said that two wars between France and England marked the beginning and the end of the age of knights and castles in Europe. The first of these wars was the Norman Conquest of England. In 1066, a duke from the Normandy region of northern France invaded and conquered England, becoming the new English king, William the Conqueror. William used knights to help win his victory, and the Normans built castles in England for protection from hostile locals. As a result, knights and castles became more popular.

Several centuries later, William's descendants claimed the legal right to the French throne. This and other causes led to the Hundred Years' War fought on French soil from 1337 to 1453. In battle after battle, French knights were defeated by English forces that included foot soldiers firing powerful longbows that filled the skies with deadly arrows.

Most of France had fallen under English control when an illiterate, teenage peasant girl appeared at the French court claiming that voices told her how to save France. That girl, Joan of Arc, led a French army to victory over the English in a battle at Orleans, France, in 1429. It was the turning point of the war. The French continued winning and finally drove the English from France in 1453. This is why Joan is loved by the French as their greatest patriot and why the English burned her at the stake.

During the Hundred Years' War, knights were made obsolete by English longbows and guns. Kings replaced knights with paid armies. Castles became obsolete because cannons could destroy stone walls. The entire feudal system was breaking down as people in England and France developed loyalties to their countries rather than to local lords. In the process, the modern nations of France and England were born.

Gothic architecture

The Roman Catholic Church reached the height of its power and influence during the late middle ages. The most visible symbol of the church's power was magnificent Gothic cathedrals built in the 1100s and 1200s including Notre Dame, Chartres, and Reims, all in France. The most prominent feature of Gothic architecture is the pointed arch, but the Gothic style is also known for soaring ceilings, walls filled with glass windows, and flying buttresses. A flying buttress is an external, arched support for the wall of a building that allowed builders to construct tall, thin, stone walls filled with colored-glass windows. Glass was extremely important to Gothic cathedrals: it lighted the interior, its beauty seemed inspired by God, and the Bible stories portrayed on the windows taught about religion at a time when most people were illiterate.

Renaissance

Renaissance means reawakening or rebirth, and it refers to a rebirth of learning from classical Greece and Rome. In the late middle ages, Italians became interested in learning about the glories of their ancestors in the Roman Empire. They searched for classical literature forgotten in monasteries, and they acquired classical works from Muslim and Byzantine scholars. Archeologists uncovered classical art and architecture.

Italians became interested in humanism, the concern with human values in this life as opposed to religious beliefs and the afterlife. Renaissance architecture abandoned the church's Gothic style and adopted the simplicity and balance of more classical forms. Artists including Michelangelo and Da Vinci shaped Western art, Shakespeare wrote plays that explored human nature, and Gutenberg's printing press spread Renaissance knowledge through cheaper books that encouraged people to learn how to read and write. The Renaissance began in Florence, Italy, about 1350 and spread to Rome and finally to much of Europe before it ended in the early 1600s. The Renaissance was a bridge between the middle ages and the modern world.

Aztecs

During the late middle ages, people of the Western Hemisphere continued to develop in isolation from the rest of the world. Agriculture had spread across much of the Americas, and Native American societies ranged from small bands of hunter-gathers to empires with millions of people. The two greatest empires of the time were the Aztec and the Inca. Both collected heavy taxes from groups they conquered.

The Aztecs were a fierce and warlike people of central and southern Mexico who controlled their subjects through fear and military force. Their polytheistic religion practiced human sacrifice on a scale unknown elsewhere in history. The Aztecs believed that their sun god required blood from beating human hearts each night in order to rise again in the morning. Often the purpose of war was to obtain victims for sacrifice. The Aztecs built their capital on swampy marshland in what is now Mexico City. Floating gardens provided the city's food. When Europeans first saw the capital, they were amazed to find an island city of 200,000 people—as big as any city in Europe—with tall temples, a huge marketplace, ball courts, and even a zoo.

Incas

The Inca civilization was centered in present-day Peru, but it grew to include most of the Pacific coast of South America between the Andes Mountains and the ocean. It was a high-altitude civilization; farmers developed irrigation systems and stepped terraces for growing crops on steep hillsides. The 3,000 mile-long Inca Empire was linked by the most extensive road system since the Roman Empire. Way stations built on main roads provided travelers with places to stay at the end of each day's journey. The Incas did not have writing as we know it, but they kept accurate numerical records on knotted strings called quipu (KEE-pu).

People living in the Americas, including the Aztecs and Incas, had no way of knowing their long separation from Eurasia was about to end, with consequences they could hardly imagine.

the great voyages of discovery

As the year 1500 approached, the world faced a turning point in history, but none were yet aware of it. Sailing ships and navigation technology had improved to a point that ships could sail anywhere in the world. The Eastern and Western Hemispheres still did not know that the other existed, but the time had come for them to meet. Who would make the introduction? Three civilizations had the necessary wealth and knowledge. The Islamic world was one of them, but it was weakened by the Mongol conquests, and it was preoccupied with local and regional matters. The Chinese civilization was another, but it had withdrawn from ocean exploration to deal with internal concerns. Only Christian Europe seemed eager to reach outward.

Europeans were hungry to explore. The Vikings had taught them how to sail the stormy Atlantic. The Crusades whetted their appetite for travel and adventure, and Marco Polo got them thinking about Asia. Europe also had the means to explore. The Renaissance brought European culture to a level of other advanced civilizations, and it gave Europeans a new sense of confidence. The competing kings of Europe were busy adopting new technologies and trade links to give them advantages over rival monarchs.

In August 1492, Spain sent Christopher Columbus into the Atlantic Ocean with three small ships to search for a western trade route to the spice islands of Asia, a voyage that finally connected the Eastern and Western Hemispheres. Sailing for Portugal, Vasco de Gama rounded Africa and connected Europe to the Indian Ocean and Asia in 1498. In 1522, Magellan's Spanish expedition circled the earth and connected the world. The world would never be the same. The middle ages were over, and modern times had begun.

Some questions to consider:

Consider Spain's decision to send Christopher Columbus to the spice lands of Asia and the Ming decision to stop ocean exploration. How do these decisions illustrate the "Law of Unintended Consequences?"

Consider the Persian invasions of ancient Greece, conquests by the Roman Empire, the Crusades, and the victories of the Mongol Empire; what can these events tell us about the long-term success of military invasions of distant lands?

The Bedside Book of World History

Part 2
1500 to the present

Chapter 7

1500s and 1600s:
The Early Modern World

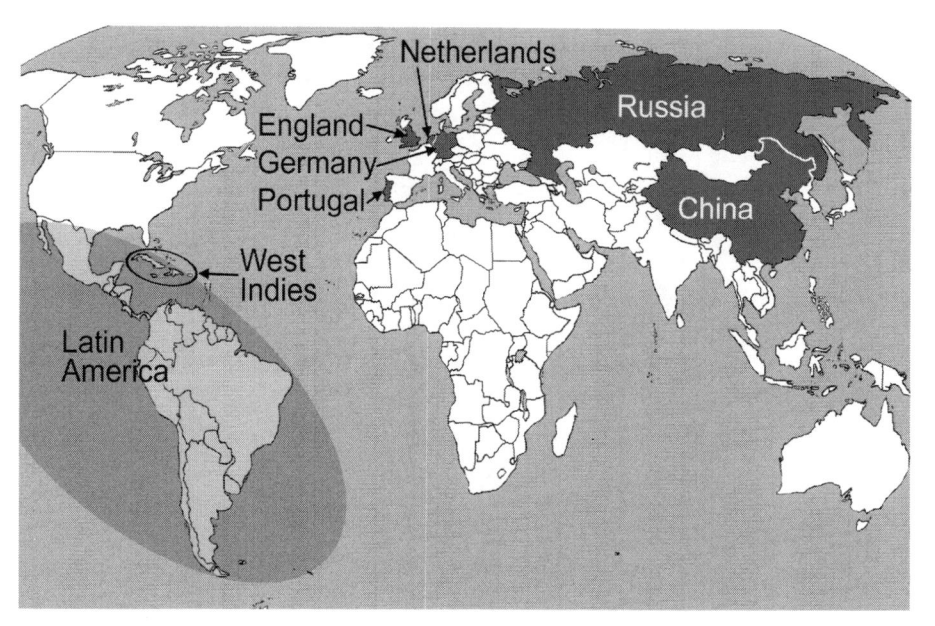

LOCATIONS: Russia, England, Germany, Portugal, Netherlands, Latin America, West Indies, China (Locations are depicted on a contemporary political map of the world.)

Preview

The "modern era" of world history began around the year 1500, when the great European voyages of discovery affected the entire world and transformed Europe into a major player on the world stage. These voyages would lead to the deaths of most Native Americans and the enslavement of Africans kidnapped from their homes to work in the silver mines and plantations of the New World.

Also, in the early modern period, a German goldsmith would change how the world communicated, and a German priest would begin a movement that tore apart the Christian world.

the Modern World

The great European voyages of discovery ushered in a new age of history, the modern age that continues to the present day. This was the first truly global age, when ships from Europe sailed the world's oceans, bringing together the Old World and the New. The consequences were enormous: Populations in the Americas were destroyed and replaced by newcomers from distant lands, international trade swelled, and people the world over started growing new plants and eating new foods.

Why did these ships come from Western Europe and not from some other advanced civilization? The Muslim world was dealing with internal concerns following the disruptions of the Mongol conquests. China was also looking inward after halting the ocean voyages of Zheng He. Kings in Western Europe, on the other hand, encouraged exploration to find new trading opportunities to increase their wealth and to help them compete against rival kings.

When the Muslim Ottomans took control in the Middle East and disturbed overland trade routes, both Spain and Portugal sent explorers to look for new ocean routes to the spice-growing lands of Asia. While Spain stumbled across America instead, Portugal succeeded in opening a southern trade route to Asia by sailing around Africa into the Indian Ocean.

With their long reach into the oceans, European nations went from being a quarrelsome collection of medieval states to the world's most dynamic civilization, still quarrelsome but armed with advanced ships and weapons. From this point forward, Western civilization and world history were bound together.

Conquest of the Americas

When Christopher Columbus and his three small ships arrived in the West Indies on an October day in 1492, they set in motion a chain of events that would profoundly change life in the Americas and elsewhere in the world. The great Aztec and Inca civilizations would soon perish, conquered by Spanish conquistadors—adventurers seeking gold and glory. The Native Americans had no weapons to match Spanish swords and cavalry.

Between 80 and 95 percent of the Americans would die and be replaced by immigrants from Europe seeking new opportunities and by immigrants from Africa who arrived in chains. Gold and silver taken from the Americas would make Spanish and Portuguese kings rich and powerful.

Chapter 7 – 1500s and 1600s: The Early Modern World

Columbian Exchange

Because Eurasia and America developed in isolation from each other for thousands of years, they had different plants and animals. After Columbus connected the two landmasses, an exchange of products began: It was called the Columbian Exchange. At this time, Native American cultures included excellent farmers who raised corn, potatoes, tomatoes, chocolate, peanuts, coffee, and tobacco. Corn and potatoes from the New World had a big impact on Chinese and European diets, leading to large population increases in both places.

The most important food America acquired from Europe was wheat, used for making bread, pasta, and the like. Soon oats, barley, grapes, rice, and sugarcane were being grown in America. Domesticated animals from Europe changed America in a big way. The plains Indians of North America, for example, built a lifestyle around horses, the Navajos around sheep, and cows came to outnumber people.

The import from Europe with the greatest impact, however, was disease. Most diseases come from human contact with animals, and Europeans had long lived closely with their horses, pigs, cows, and sheep, animals that did not exist in the Americas. Over centuries, Europeans developed some immunity to diseases like smallpox and measles. Native Americans had no such immunity. When these diseases arrived in America, indigenous (native) populations were largely wiped out, emptying much of the land for Europeans.

capitalism (or the free market)

The voyages of discovery shifted the focus of European trade from the Mediterranean Sea to the Atlantic coast. Venice declined as a major trade center, while port cities prospered in Portugal and Spain followed by England, France, and the Netherlands (the Dutch). To increase their income from taxes on foreign trade, European monarchs encouraged the formation of joint-stock companies. Stock (or shares) was sold to several investors who shared the risk of expensive ocean trading voyages. If a ship went down, no single investor lost everything, but if a voyage was successful, all stockholders shared in the profits. Most voyages succeeded, and many investors made good money. The modern stock market operates in a similar way today.

Best known of these companies were the British East India Company that traded mostly with India and the Dutch East India Company that operated in Southeast and East Asia. Both acted as extensions of their governments and even had their own armies. Joint stock companies promoted the rise of an economic system called capitalism (or the free market).

Capital is wealth such as ships, factories, or money. Under capitalism, people are free to own capital and make their own decisions about how to use it. Since joint-stock companies were chartered by governments, they were a form of state-sponsored capitalism.

Atlantic slave trade

A capitalist economic system can benefit society by producing the best possible products at the lowest possible prices due to competition among producers. But with companies focused on making the best possible profits, capitalism can sometimes harm people. The African slave trade was one example.

After the discovery of America, European countries began sending people to the New World to establish colonies to produce goods for trade. With native populations dying off, Europe looked for another source of cheap labor. Although slavery no longer existed in Europe, Europeans began importing slaves from Africa to work on plantations and mines in the New World. Before this time, most African slaves had been enemies captured in battle. But, as the slave trade grew, Africans began kidnapping other Africans in large numbers and selling them to European slave traders.

Due to ocean currents and prevailing "trade winds," European sailors learned that they could make the fastest crossing to America by first sailing south to Africa. On the last leg of this Triangular Trade Route, the Gulf Stream ocean current sped ships from America back to Europe. Leaving West Africa for America on the "Middle Passage" of this three-part journey, ship cargo holds were crammed full of Africa's chief export, human beings. Conditions on the slave ships were appalling. Many slaves died of disease from eating rotten food and breathing foul air. Some desperate slaves took their own lives. When these African people were sold at slave markets in the New World, the profits were used to purchase plantation products such as sugar, coffee, tobacco, and cotton, which were shipped back to Europe and sold there. It was a splendid system of trade for everyone except the Africans whose lives were ruined.

New Spain

The Atlantic powers of Europe came to dominate trade on the world's oceans. Portugal's trading empire included Brazil in South America and trading stations in Africa and Asia. The huge Spanish trading empire stretched from Europe to Asia to the Americas. Spain's holdings in America were called New Spain; they extended from what is now the southern U.S. to the tip of South America. (Today, lands south of the

U.S. are called Latin America.) New Spain's biggest business enterprise was silver mining, which produced enough silver to make Spain the most powerful nation in Europe, if not in the world.

Unlike English settlers in North America, who maintained a distance from the "Indians," the Spanish wanted to bring the indigenous people of New Spain into the Catholic faith. Many Spaniards intermarried with Native Americans and later with African Americans, creating a distinctive new civilization in Latin America. In this mixed society, Spaniards born in Europe were at the top of the social pyramid followed by Spaniards born in America (creoles). These people controlled society in New Spain. Next in rank were people of mixed Spanish and Native American heritage (mestizos) and mixed Spanish and black heritage (mulattos). At the bottom of society were Native Americans and African Americans of unmixed ancestry.

Qing Dynasty (CHING)

During the early modern period, China's Ming Dynasty tried to isolate itself from Western cultural influences; only two Chinese ports were open to European ships. Still, Chinese products were so popular in Europe that much of the Spanish silver mined in the New World ended up in China, where it paid for Chinese silks, tea, and fine porcelain. The Ming dynasty began requiring Chinese to pay their taxes in silver. When harsh weather reduced harvests, peasants didn't have enough food or enough silver. It is said starving peasants ate goose droppings and tree bark. Disease and death swept through China.

The Ming government was weak after years of internal conflicts, and it was unable to contend with large peasant uprisings. As soldiers from a peasant army climbed the walls of the Forbidden City, the last Ming emperor hung himself in 1644. Like others before it, the Ming Dynasty grew, flowered, declined, and was replaced. The new rulers would be **Manchu** nomads from northeast of the Great Wall, a region known as Manchuria. They entered China, defeated the peasant army, and established the Qing Dynasty that endured for two-and-a-half centuries until the early 1900s. The Qing Dynasty would be China's last.

Tokugawa Shogunate

During the late middle ages, Japan suffered through a long period of internal wars. Japan was divided into many kingdoms; warlords lived in fortresses, and they employed mounted samurai warriors. It looked a lot like the feudal system of the middle ages in Europe.

Endless warfare and pillaging made life miserable for Japanese peasants. Then in the mid-1500s, something happened to change all this: Portuguese traders showed up in Japan selling firearms. With the help of guns, a series of three warlords succeeded in conquering and unifying Japan. The last of these warlords, Tokugawa, became Japan's shogun, or military ruler, in 1603. The shogunate adopted a Japanese version of Confucianism, and it improved education in Japan.

Concerned about the intentions and the influence of Europeans, the Tokugawa Shogunate adopted a policy of near total isolation from the West. Japan expelled Christian missionaries, burned Western books, and allowed only the Chinese and Dutch to trade with Japan at just one port. The southern port city of Nagasaki became Japan's only window on the outside world.

Peter the Great

Russia emerged as a great power during the early modern period. In 1480, under the leadership of Ivan III, duke of Moscow, Russia finally threw off the Mongol domination that had long crippled Russia's development. Ivan tripled the size of Russian territory and rebuilt Moscow's fortress, the Kremlin, which is still home to Russia's rulers. Ivan declared himself the first Russian czar, or Caesar. He is now known as Ivan the Great. Russia continued to grow in size as later czars encouraged peasants to move into new territories. With the help of firearms, Russian settlers spread across the steppes of central Asia, finally putting an end to the military superiority of mounted nomadic warriors. Russian territory eventually reached the Pacific Ocean, creating an empire of many ethnic groups—the largest in the world.

In 1682, Russia got a new and energetic czar who stood nearly seven feet tall. He was Peter I, known as Peter the Great. Peter took eighteen months off to travel as a commoner in Europe, where he worked as a carpenter and learned about the West. Peter tried to bring Russia into the modern world by adopting elements of Western culture and technology. He imported printing presses along with European clothing and architecture, and he adopted the Western calendar. Peter also reorganized his military and civil service along European lines. In a war with Sweden, Peter acquired land on the Baltic Sea, giving Russia an ocean outlet to the west and direct access to Europe by ship. There he built a European-style capital at St. Petersburg. Peter died at the age of 53 after jumping into icy water to save drowning sailors.

Chapter 7 – 1500s and 1600s: The Early Modern World

Gutenberg

Big things were happening in Europe during the early modern period: the Renaissance was spreading from Italy to northern Europe, major scientific discoveries were being made, Christianity was breaking apart, and a German jeweler improved on Chinese printing techniques to change how the world communicated.

As a goldsmith, Johann Gutenberg was skilled at working with small pieces of metal. He combined this skill with an olive press design to produce a new printing press that used metal movable type. After his press printed multiple copies of one page, the pieces of type were reused to print more pages.

Before this, it took a person anywhere from six months to two years to copy one book by hand. Gutenberg's press made printing much faster, so books became less expensive and more widely available. People now had a reason to learn how to read and write. As a result, the printing press greatly expanded literacy, and it spread news of scientific discoveries and Renaissance ideas to wider audiences.

Protestant Reformation

Without Gutenberg's press, we might not remember the name Martin Luther. But through the power of the press, Luther's ideas spread until they tore apart the Catholic Church. The influence of the church had already started to decline during the late middle ages following the horror of the Black Death and conflicts over who was the rightful pope. Then, along came the Renaissance to revive the classical Greek idea of humanism, a concern with human life on earth that further reduced the influence of the church.

But the biggest blow to the Roman Catholic Church came in 1517, when Luther, a Catholic monk and college professor, nailed his "95 Theses" (or arguments) to the door of a Catholic Church in Germany. Luther was upset about the sale of "indulgences," which allowed Catholics to pay money to be forgiven of sins. The money was being used to build the huge, new, Renaissance-style St. Peter's Basilica in Rome.

Luther also believed that every person could have a direct relationship with God, so there was little need for Catholic priests or Catholic rituals. The printing press made such a direct relationship easier by supplying Bibles in local languages, not just in Latin. People could now read the Bible for themselves.

Luther's attempt to *reform* the Catholic Church is called the Reformation. His *protest* led to the establishment of Protestant churches, a new branch of Christianity. The Protestant Reformation not only fractured the church; it opened minds to new ways of thinking. If it was now possible to question the sacred teachings of mother church, it might also be possible to question other long-held beliefs about science, politics, and society.

Counter-Reformation

At about this time, the Catholic Church was adopting reforms of its own. A new Catholic religious order, the Jesuits, promoted education and sent missionaries to Asia and America. Schools were opened to educate women in Renaissance learning, and the sale of indulgences was stopped. This Counter-Reformation, or Catholic Reformation, had another important task: fighting the ideas of Protestantism.

The Counter-Reformation identified books to be burned, and it stepped up the work of the Inquisition, a system of church courts that placed heretics and sinners on trial. Torture and imprisonment were used to extract confessions from Protestants and disobedient Catholics. The Inquisition was especially strong in Spain, where Christian forces had only recently succeeded in pushing the Muslim Moors back to North Africa. For centuries under Muslim rule, Spain had been a multicultural society where Muslims, Jews, and Christians lived side by side. After Christians retook Spain in 1492 (called the "Reconquista"), Jews and Muslims were expelled from Spain.

Elizabeth I

England became a Protestant country in 1534 when King Henry VIII broke from the Catholic Church so he could divorce his first wife and marry Anne Boleyn. He was hoping for a male heir, but instead they had a daughter. His daughter grew up to become one of history's most brilliant rulers, Queen Elizabeth I. Elizabeth was intelligent and confident. By tolerating religious differences, she maintained peace in her kingdom. She ruled for nearly a half century during the Renaissance in England, the "Elizabethan Period," when William Shakespeare wrote his plays, and the English language underwent rapid development. Greek and Latin words entered the English vocabulary, and Shakespeare alone invented hundreds of new words.

It was during Elizabeth's reign that England defeated the "invincible" Spanish Armada of 130 warships sent by Spain to attack and invade England. Although Spain was the world's largest empire, England and France were also building navies to compete on the oceans. Spain's Catholic king wanted to conquer the meddlesome English and return

England to the Catholic faith. As the Armada waited off the French coast for its invasion army to arrive, the British sent burning fire ships against the Spanish vessels, forcing them to scatter. With their battle formation broken, the Spanish ships were unable to fend off the smaller, faster, and more maneuverable British warships with their longer-range cannons. The defeat of the Armada in 1588 was a huge blow to Spain's pride and confidence, and it made England ruler of the waves.

Wars of Religion

Conflicts between Protestants and Catholics in Europe escalated until the two sides went to war in the 1500s and fought for more than a hundred years. With both sides convinced God was on their side, the fighting was especially bloody. Religion wasn't the only issue involved; some rulers used the religious wars as an opportunity to seek advantage against rival powers. The last of the religious wars was the Thirty Years' War, which involved nearly every country in Europe. By the time it was over, one-third of Germany was dead, and Europe lay devastated. The killing of Christians by Christians had resulted in the worst disaster since the Black Death, but this disaster was created by humans.

At the end of the war, the Treaty of Westphalia (1648) decreed that the ruler of each kingdom could choose the religion for his own land. Southern Europe (France, Italy, Spain) chose to remain with the Roman Catholic Church, while northern Europe (such as Germany, England, and Scandinavia) generally chose to be Protestant, a pattern that remains with us today. As another consequence of the Thirty Years' War, France replaced Spain as the strongest country in Europe.

divine right monarchs

European kings grew extremely powerful during the early modern period for several reasons: Kingdoms had grown wealthy from trade to Asia and the Americas; international trade required big merchant fleets and strong navies; and after a century of religious warfare, Europeans looked to strong monarchs to maintain stability. Monarchs claimed to rule with a "divine right" that came directly from God. The grandest of the divine right monarchs was Louis XIV (LOO-ee the 14th) who called himself the "Sun King." He ruled France for 72-years when France was at the height of its power (1643–1715).

Twelve miles outside Paris, Louis built a palace fit for a god-king. His huge palace at Versailles (vur-SIGH) was surrounded by endless gardens and 1,500 fountains. Versailles was built in an artistic style called Baroque (buh-ROKE), which replaced the classical-style art of the Renaissance.

Baroque art was complex and dazzling; it was filled with ornamentation and gold. It was art meant to impress all who saw it with the power and wealth of the king or the church. Other rulers tried to copy the splendor of Versailles, but none ever equaled it. Louis shrewdly used his court at Versailles to control the French nobility. As many as 5,000 French nobles living at Versailles had little to do except seek the king's favor and compete for honors like holding the candle while the Sun King prepared for bed.

Scientific Revolution

The Renaissance, the Reformation, the discovery of new lands—all these events opened European minds to new ways of thinking, and this included the pursuit of science. Galileo of Italy used a telescope to observe the heavens and prove the Earth was not the center of the universe. (The Catholic Church disagreed and locked him up.) Isaac Newton of England discovered the principle of gravity while sitting under an apple tree; he concluded that all objects in the universe obey the same laws of motion.

A Dutch shopkeeper and amateur scientist, Anton von Leeuwenhoek (LAY-vun-hook), built an early microscope and was struck with "wonder at a thousand living creatures in one drop of water." This new world of tiny organisms challenged the accepted theory of spontaneous generation, a theory that proposed small creatures such as insects spring to life from rocks or air. Leeuwenhoek suspected eggs.

These and other discoveries amounted to a leap in scientific understanding in the 1600s that came to be called the Scientific Revolution. Printed books spread this new scientific knowledge along with the revolutionary idea that the workings of the universe could be explained by natural causes.

Some questions to consider:

How can the capitalist economic system be good for people when it works well? How can the capitalist system sometimes harm people?

How does the early modern period demonstrate that trade has been a major force in world history?

If religions are supposed to make people better people, what can explain why conflicts over religion have been so deadly in history?

Chapter 8

1700s:
Enlightenment and Revolution

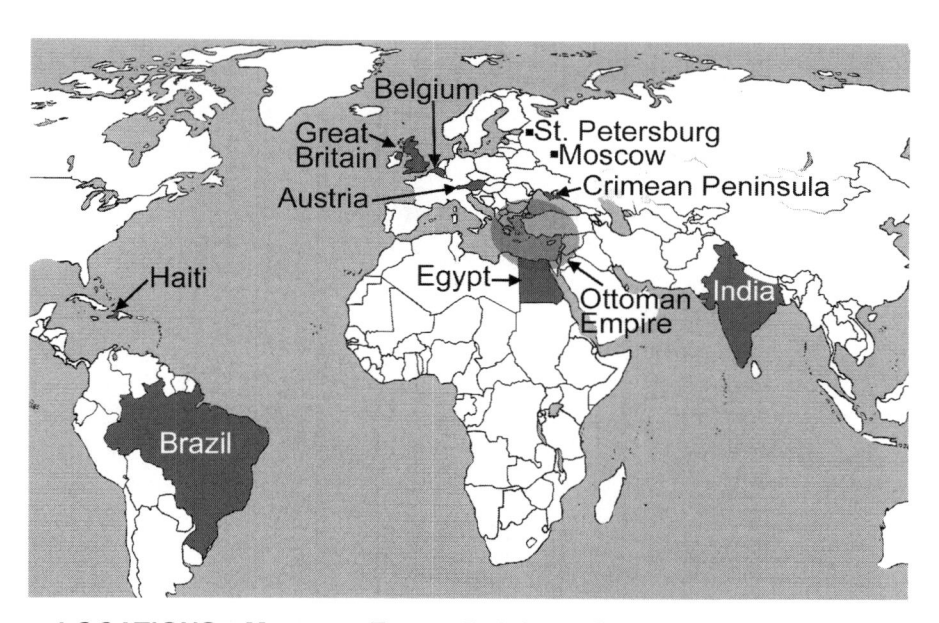

LOCATIONS: Moscow, Egypt, Belgium, Great Britain, Austria, Brazil, Haiti, St. Petersburg, Crimean Peninsula, India, Ottoman Empire (Locations are depicted on a contemporary political map of the world.)

Preview

During the 1700s, many educated people in Europe and the Americas started to see the world in a new light; it was called the "Enlightenment." Although kings had ruled countries for thousands of years, Enlightenment thinkers asked, "What gives kings the right to rule others?"

Enlightenment philosophers suggested radical new ways to organize society around ideas like freedom, equality, and democracy, ideas that inspired revolutions that ended the rule of kings in the United States, France, and Latin America.

the Enlightenment

The big lesson of the Scientific Revolution was that "natural laws" governed the operation of the universe—not God, superstition, witchcraft, or mysterious forces like spontaneous generation. Furthermore, these natural laws could be discovered by using reason. Writers and thinkers began to take these lessons from science, the physical world, and apply them to society, the world of people.

During this new "Age of Reason," philosophers like John Locke in England and Voltaire in France claimed the power to rule came from the people, not from a divine right. They asked if nations should be ruled by monarchs who came to power through an accident of birth. They wrote of "self-evident truths" that required more democratic forms of government and "natural laws" that made all people equal. French philosopher Jean Jacques Rousseau wrote, "Man is born free, and everywhere he is in chains." Rousseau said the ruler had a social contract with the people. If a ruler didn't do what was best for the people, he violated the contract, and the people had a right to overthrow him.

Old ideas like serfdom and absolute monarchy were considered leftovers from the outdated ancien régime (old regime, old system). Many educated people rejected traditional religion, becoming Deists who believed in God and morality but did not accept church authority, church rituals, or beliefs that disagreed with science. These new ideas about reason, freedom, and equality are called the Enlightenment.

Adam Smith

Enlightenment thinking wasn't limited to politics; it extended to other areas of society such as economics and women's rights. In 1776, Scottish philosopher Adam Smith published an influential book called The Wealth of Nations; it is considered the first full explanation of the capitalist economic system. Smith said rulers should stop trying to control their nations' economies. Economies would work best, he said, if they were left alone to control themselves through the "invisible hand" of competition in a free market. Smith's belief came to be known as laissez faire (LES-ay-fair), French for "leave it alone."

English writer Mary Wollstonecraft believed Enlightenment ideas about equality should apply to women as well as men. Her book A Vindication of the Rights of Woman, proposed that educational systems be reformed to give girls the same education as boys. Her controversial ideas had little immediate effect, but they became a foundation for the women's rights movement that would arise in the next century.

Chapter 8 – 1700s: Enlightenment and Revolution

American Revolution

Enlightenment ideas found fertile ground in the British colonies of America, where influential leaders such as Benjamin Franklin, Thomas Jefferson, and George Washington were Enlightenment thinkers and Deists. Americans felt Britain had violated the social contract by passing unfair laws, so Americans were justified in throwing off British rule. The American Revolution in 1776 made a big impression on many people in Europe who saw it as a turning point in history; Americans had enforced the social contract, ended rule by the king, and established the first national democracy since ancient times.

The Declaration of Independence, written largely by Jefferson, began with a restatement of the Enlightenment ideas of philosopher John Locke: "We hold these truths to be self-evident, that all men are created equal, that they are endowed by their Creator with certain unalienable Rights, that among these are Life, Liberty and the pursuit of Happiness." By demonstrating that Enlightenment ideas could be used to govern a nation, the young democracy in America became the model for a better world.

the Third Estate

Although France was a birthplace of Enlightenment thinking, France was still living under the ancien régime. Society was made up of three classes called estates. The First Estate was the clergy (church officials), and the Second Estate was the nobility. The clergy and nobles made up only two percent of the population, but they owned one-third of the land, and they paid few taxes. Everyone else belonged to the Third Estate, the commoner class in France. They paid the taxes that financed France's government.

The commoners of the large Third Estate included rural peasants, the urban poor, artisans, and the middle class. The middle class, or bourgeoisie (burzh-wah-zee), was made up of successful and educated people like large landowners, merchants, doctors, lawyers, scholars, and government officials. They had wealth and economic power and paid taxes, but they had little say in government. In America, it was the middle class who led the revolution against England; in France the middle class was growing restless too.

In 1789, King Louis XVI (the Sun King's great-great-great-grandson) called representatives from France's three estates to the palace at Versailles for a meeting of the Estates General, an old institution from medieval times that had met only once in the past three centuries. The king needed cash.

French Revolution

France was deeply in debt from supporting the American Revolution against the British, France's old enemy. King Louis XVI convened the Estates General to discuss raising taxes. Representatives from the Third Estate, mostly bourgeoisie, knew they would be outvoted by the other two estates and be stuck paying the new taxes. Frustrated, the Third Estate declared it was the nation's new legislature, the "National Assembly." When locked out of their meeting room, the Assembly met on a tennis court and swore an oath not to go home until France had a modern constitution. The king called out the army.

In 1789, France was ripe for revolution. Not only were the bourgeoisie angry about having little say in government, the peasants and urban poor were hungry after two years of bad harvests. As the king's troops marched toward Versailles, the enraged people of Paris stormed and captured the Bastille, a prison that represented the ancien régime. (Bastille Day, July 14, is France's independence day.)

The French Revolution was underway. The Paris mob executed the mayor and paraded his head through the streets on a pole. Throughout the countryside, peasants attacked the nobility and burned feudal documents. The National Assembly abolished feudalism in France, and in the streets the common people shouted, "Liberté, Egalité, Fraternité!" (Liberty, Equality, Brotherhood). Hungry women armed themselves and marched to Versailles; they forced the king to return to Paris, where they placed him under house arrest.

Reign of Terror

Many of France's nobles fled to other countries where they encouraged foreign kings to stop the French Revolution before it could spread. France was soon at war with Prussia and Austria, later joined by Britain, Spain, and the Netherlands. France drafted all able-bodied men into the military and raised an army of nearly one million men. With foreign armies invading French territory, economic problems in Paris, and fears about enemies within France, a group of radicals took control of the revolution.

The radicals took extreme measures against their enemies, real or imagined. After the king and queen were caught attempting to flee from France, they were marched to the guillotine and beheaded. Members of the nobility and the clergy were beheaded. The radicals even beheaded other revolutionaries. Some 50,000 people died during France's bloody "Reign of Terror," about half at the guillotine.

Chapter 8 – 1700s: Enlightenment and Revolution

Napoleon

After the French army managed to eliminate the immediate threat of foreign invasion, new leaders took control in France and ended the Reign of Terror. Still, the government was unable to end foreign wars or improve the economy, and the army was frequently called in to maintain order. In 1799, a brilliant young general named Napoleon Bonaparte seized control of France.

Napoleon was a popular leader. After military victories in Italy, he proclaimed himself emperor and began his conquest of Europe. Napoleon's army was unique: French soldiers believed in their cause of spreading the Revolution, and the army chose its officers based on ability, not on noble birth. Leading a capable, dedicated, and battle-hardened army, Napoleon easily defeated all forces sent against him.

In the lands he conquered, Napoleon eliminated feudalism and serfdom, improved education, and promoted the arts and sciences. He established a uniform legal system, the Napoleonic Code, that guaranteed freedom of religion and granted equal rights to all men. The Code, however, reduced gains made by women during the revolution. Women would have to wait another century for their equality.

Neoclassical art and Classical music

In Europe, divine right, absolute monarchy, and the ancien régime were swept away by the Enlightenment, revolution, and Napoleon. A simpler artistic style was needed to replace the rich and fancy Baroque style of the god-kings. Again the Western world turned to classical Greece and Rome for artistic inspiration; the new style was termed "Neoclassical," meaning "new classical."

Emperor Napoleon considered himself the new Caesar of the new Rome. He had himself crowned in the style of Roman emperors. He built classical-style monuments such as the Arc de Triomphe in Paris, and he spread Neoclassicism to the countries he conquered. Meanwhile, the young republic in the United States chose Neoclassical architecture for its new capital in Washington, D.C. Other changes were also happening in the art world: successful members of the middle class now bought art, not just kings and churches. And artists were learning their skills at "academies," not through the support of rich patrons.

While the art and architecture of the period are called Neoclassical, the music is simply called Classical because ancient classical music had not survived to claim that name. Classical music originated with opera, which was meant to imitate ancient Greek theater. Classical music replaced the Baroque musical style popular at the court of France's Louis XIV and other kings.

This was Europe's greatest age of music; it was centered in Vienna, Austria, where music was the focus of upper-class social life. During a remarkable 50-year period (1775–1825), Classical music giants Haydn, (HIGH-dun) Beethoven, and Mozart worked side by side in the same city. "Papa" Haydn gave encouragement to Mozart and lessons to Beethoven. Musicians flocked to Vienna, where they found training, jobs, money, honor, and fame.

Horatio Nelson

England was the only major European power not conquered by Napoleon, due largely to the British naval victory at Trafalgar. In 1805, a combined French and Spanish fleet of 33 warships was intercepted by a British fleet of 27 ships under the command of Admiral Horatio Nelson, a most uncommon sailor. Wounded in a naval battle ten years earlier, Nelson lost the use of his right eye. In a sea battle three years after that, he lost his right arm. The following year, Nelson defeated a French fleet at "The Battle of the Nile," forcing Napoleon to withdraw from Egypt. Three years after that, he was in a battle against a Dutch fleet when the British commander gave the signal to withdraw. Nelson put the telescope to his blind eye and said he could see no such signal. Nelson went on to destroy the Dutch fleet.

The Battle of Trafalgar would be Nelson's greatest victory and his last. Before the battle, he told his sailors "England expects that every man will do his duty." Nelson's ships engaged the larger enemy fleet at Cape Trafalgar off the southwest coast of Spain. When the smoke cleared, 20 French and Spanish ships had been destroyed or captured without the loss of a single British vessel. Nelson, however, was shot by a French sniper and died aboard his flagship, HMS *Victory*. Before he died, Nelson was certain of victory, and he declared, "Thank God I have done my duty." Trafalgar wrecked Napoleon's plans to invade England, and Britain continued to rule the waves for another hundred years. Today a statue of Admiral Nelson stands atop a tall column in London's main square, Trafalgar Square.

Haiti

One of France's richest colonies was Haiti in the West Indies. Its wealth was based on a brutal slave economy. Slaves in the Americas often resisted their masters by running away or fighting back. In Haiti, slaves succeeded in taking over a country. When the turmoil of the French Revolution spilled over to Haiti, slaves used the opportunity to revolt. Under the leadership of Toussaint-Louverture, slaves took control in Haiti, defeated an invasion force sent by Britain, and freed all slaves on the island.

When Louverture heard that France planned to return and reinstate slavery, he wrote, "Do they think that men who have been able to enjoy the blessing of liberty will calmly see it snatched away?" In 1802, Napoleon sent a large army to Haiti to restore French control and slavery. Loverture was captured and died in a French prison. Soon, however, the French were defeated by a combination of yellow fever and Haitian rebel fighters. Haiti became the second nation in the Americas, after the U.S., to gain independence. Haiti's slave revolt worried slave owners, but it was a symbol of hope to blacks.

Napoleon's invasion of Russia

Napoleon's downfall began with his biggest military mistake, an attempt to invade and conquer the vast empire of Russia. The Russians had no hope of defeating Napoleon's huge and powerful Grand Army of more than 600,000 soldiers, the largest army ever assembled in Europe. So the Russians burned everything in Napoleon's path to deny his army food and shelter. After a bloody but indecisive battle at Borodino, Napoleon captured the Russian capital of Moscow, but it was nearly empty. Knowing that his army could not survive the coming winter in Russia, Napoleon had to retreat. As the Grand Army made its way back to France, temperatures dropped to 30 degrees below zero during the bitter-cold Russian winter of 1812. Between the cold, starvation, Russian attacks, and desertion, only 30,000 of Napoleon's original soldiers returned to France. It was one of the worst disasters in military history.

Disgraced by the ruin of his Grand Army, then defeated in battles by an alliance of European nations, Napoleon was captured and forced into exile on the small island of Elba off the coast of Italy. It wasn't long, however, before Napoleon escaped and returned to France, where he raised another army. Napoleon met his final defeat at the hands of a British-led allied army near the town of Waterloo, Belgium, in 1815. Again Napoleon was exiled, this time to St. Helena, a remote British island in the South Atlantic, where he died in 1821, probably of stomach cancer or arsenic poisoning.

Simon Bolívar

Inspired by revolutions in America and France, people of Latin America wanted independence too. A creole named Simon Bolívar led the way. Bolívar was born in 1783 to a wealthy family in Venezuela. After studying Enlightenment ideas at home and in Europe, Bolívar returned to Venezuela and raised an army to fight for independence from Spain. With Spain preoccupied by the Napoleonic Wars, Bolívar achieved victory in his native Venezuela, and then went on to defeat the Spanish in what is now Colombia, Ecuador, and Bolivia.

Bolívar's final victory in Peru ended Spanish rule in South America. Bolivar failed, however, in his dream of bringing South America together in a union. Although he died a discouraged man, Bolívar is remembered as "The Liberator," and the country of Bolivia is named in his honor.

At the same time Bolívar was fighting for South American independence in the early 1800s, Mexico and countries in Central America were also fighting for their independence from Spain. Meanwhile, Brazil declared its independence from Portugal. In a period of just twenty years, the three-hundred-year European domination of Latin America came to an end.

British Parliament

In contrast to revolutions in the United States, France, and Latin America that lasted only a few years, revolution against the monarchy in England was a long, slow process that took centuries to unfold. It began in 1215, when the "Great Council" of English nobles forced King John to sign the Magna Carta, a document that established the principle that the king was not above the law. The Magna Carta was an early step toward the kind of constitutional government later established in the United States, France, and other democracies.

Over time, the Great Council evolved into a lawmaking body called Parliament. When an English king interfered with religious practices in the mid-1600s, Parliament raised an army that defeated and executed the king. In the late 1600s, Parliament removed another king from power and replaced him with a king and queen who agreed to follow a "Bill of Rights" strongly influenced by the Enlightenment views of John Locke. Although the British monarch continued to serve as head of state, Parliament has been the true power in Great Britain since the 1700s. England was not yet a democracy, however, because the nobility controlled Parliament, and few people had the right to vote.

Catherine the Great

Several weak emperors ruled Russia after the death of Peter the Great. One was Peter III, who married a lively German princess named Catherine who was anything but weak. In fact, it's commonly believed she approved Peter's murder in 1762. Although Catherine's son was next in line for the throne, she pushed him aside and ruled Russia as empress. In some respects, Catherine continued the Westernization program begun by Peter the Great. She imported farming and manufacturing techniques from the West along with European art. Enlightenment philosophers were her friends.

But trouble was brewing in the empire. Hardship caused by war with the Ottomans joined with plague to make life especially hard for Russian peasants (called serfs). They rose up in the greatest revolt yet seen in Russia. After putting down the rebellion, Catherine abandoned her Enlightenment philosophies and ruled with an iron fist. She took rights away from the serfs and increased the power of their noble landlords. By the time she had finished, serfs were little more than slaves, and hardly a free peasant remained in Russia.

However, Catherine created one of the world's finest art museums at the Hermitage in St. Petersburg, and she expanded the Russian Empire west into Poland. After her armies defeated the weakening Ottoman Empire, Russia took control of the Crimean peninsula on the Black Sea, which gave Russia direct access to the Mediterranean and a warm-water port that could stay open year round. Under Catherine's forceful rule, Russia grew strong and was capable of challenging other great powers. For these reasons she earned the title "Catherine the Great."

Mughal Empire

Back in the 1300s, when *Mongol* control over India weakened, India broke into many states. Two centuries later, Muslim invaders armed with firearms conquered northern India and established the Mughal Empire, the last of India's golden ages. The great Mughal ruler Akbar practiced religious tolerance toward India's Hindu majority; he even married a Hindu princess. Trade and agriculture flourished; India exported millions of yards of inexpensive cotton cloth that clothed much of Europe.

A much-admired art style emerged from the blending of Hindu and Islamic artistic traditions. Mughal architecture reached its zenith with the Taj Mahal, a tomb built by a Mughal ruler to honor his beloved wife who died in childbirth. It is considered by many the most beautiful building in the world.

In the early 1700s, a Mughal ruler extended his empire over most of southern Asia, but the constant warfare so weakened the empire that India once again fragmented into regional states. The breakdown of Mughal authority gave Britain an opportunity to extend its commercial interests in India. In the mid-1700s, forces from the British East India Company defeated armies of the French and Dutch trading companies. Britain then fought Indian armies to take control of the Bengal region in northeastern India. The ancient and legendary land of India was fast becoming a colony of the British Empire.

gunpowder empires

After the Chinese invented gunpowder, firearms began to play a major role in world history. Gunpowder weapons helped new rulers take control in Tokugawa Japan, Mughal India, the steppes of Russia, and elsewhere. With the help of gunpowder weapons, European nations created huge trading empires.

The Portuguese were probably first to place cannons on ocean-going ships. Europeans had acquired much of their sailing technology from the East, including the compass, astrolabe, rudder, and lateen sails for sailing into the wind. The Europeans added their own improvements including better cannons and faster ships that were built strong enough to withstand the recoil of cannon fire without being shaken apart.

With shipboard cannons, Europeans pushed into the waters of Asia and Africa and came to dominate the world's oceans. Kings in Europe always had to be ready to adopt the latest in weapons technology to survive the endless conflicts among Europe's competing powers. In the next century, the 1800s, Europe's advanced weaponry would extend Western European dominance from the oceans to the land.

Some questions to consider:

Can ideas be as powerful as armies?

What did the Enlightenment philosopher Rousseau mean when he said, "Man is born free, and everywhere he is in chains."

What conditions can help a revolution to succeed?

How well does Adam Smith's "invisible hand" work in today's world?

Some people have compared the invention of the printing press to the invention of digital technology, which now makes it possible to obtain information at our fingertips and makes it possible for everyone to publish on the Internet. Is this a reasonable comparison?

Chapter 9

1800s:
Industrialism and Imperialism

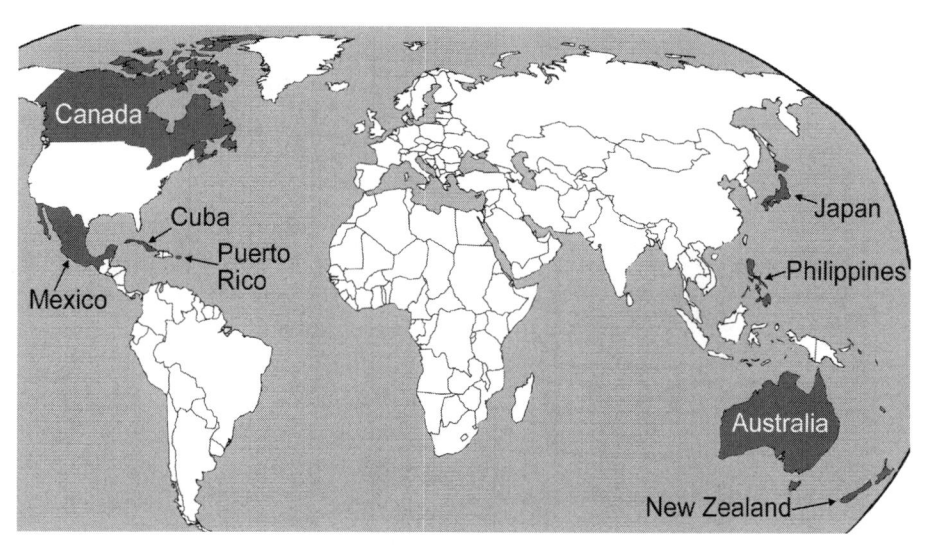

LOCATIONS: Japan, Cuba, Philippines, Canada, Australia, New Zealand, Puerto Rico, Mexico (Locations are depicted on a contemporary political map of the world.)

Preview

During the 1800s, Western nations started to power machines by burning fuels, and the Industrial Revolution was born. Products were now being made in large factories, which put many craftspeople out of work, but made goods more affordable.

People left farms for factory towns where they worked long hours for low wages under poor conditions. In response, many workers adopted the economic philosophy of socialism, which promised a more equal distribution of wealth. Other workers formed labor unions to fight for a better deal from their bosses.

Soon, Western nations would use their powerful machines to conquer much of the world.

Industrial Revolution

Midway through the modern era, people learned how to make machines move by burning fuels. The first of these machines was the steam engine that burned coal to heat water that made steam that pushed a piston that turned a wheel. Goods that had always been made by hand in homes and shops were replaced by goods made in large quantities at lower cost by machines in factories. Humans had never gone faster than horses could carry them, but now steam-powered trains and ships moved people and goods faster and cheaper than ever before. This technological revolution began in England's textile (cloth) mills in the late 1700s and spread to other Western nations during the 1800s. These new technologies would soon change how people lived, and they would determine who ruled the world.

The Industrial Revolution affected society in both positive and negative ways. Factories could produce goods more cheaply than hand labor, so people could buy more goods and enjoy a higher standard of living than before. But factories put many craftspeople out of work. Factories required large numbers of workers, which caused huge migrations of people from the countryside to the cities where they worked long hours for low wages while living in crowded and unsanitary conditions. Even small children worked as many as 16 hours a day, becoming so tired they fell into machinery and were crippled or killed.

socialism

In 50 years, the English manufacturing city of Liverpool grew from 80,000 to 375,000 people. Cities could not cope with the huge influx of workers coming to work in the factories of the Industrial Revolution. A dozen people might be crowded together in one small room in a run-down apartment building called a tenement. Due to a lack of sewage facilities, filth was everywhere, and infectious disease killed one child in four before the age of five. The Industrial Revolution was making a few people very wealthy, but countless others were poor and living under miserable conditions.

Not surprisingly, many working-class people were attracted to the ideas of socialism, an economic philosophy that called for a more even distribution of wealth. Socialism proclaimed, "From each according to his ability, to each according to his need." Under socialism, major businesses would be owned by the public, not by a few wealthy men. Socialism was basically the opposite of Adam Smith's capitalism.

Impressionism

The Industrial Revolution brought many technological marvels such as antiseptics to kill bacteria in hospitals, vaccinations to prevent disease, the telegraph, telephone, light bulb, automobile, airplane, and the camera. The camera had a big impact on the art world in the late 1800s. Since the camera could reproduce scenes from life more accurately than any artist could, artists needed to find a new mission. Rather than trying to accurately reproduce reality, artists began to paint their "impressions" of what they saw. Painters like Monet and Renoir worked quickly using short, choppy brushstrokes to form vibrant mosaics of color. Art changed radically as artists became free to put their own ideas and feelings into their works.

Impressionism marked the beginning of modern art. In architecture, the industrial age was symbolized by the Eiffel Tower, built in Paris in 1889 to celebrate the 100th anniversary of the French Revolution. At nearly 1,000 feet tall, it was an impressive demonstration of the steel and iron construction techniques of the Industrial Revolution, and it was a model for the steel-skeleton skyscrapers to come.

conservative versus liberal

Following the Napoleonic Wars, Europe was ready for a period of calm. Leaders representing the "Great Powers" of Europe met in Vienna to hammer out an agreement meant to undo changes brought about by the French Revolution and Napoleon and to maintain a lasting peace by restoring a balance of power among European nations. They sought to prevent any nation from becoming stronger than the others, as France had done under Napoleon. Delegates to the Congress of Vienna were members of the aristocracy (upper class), who wanted a return to the old order in which monarchs and the upper class controlled a stable society. People who resist change and try to preserve traditional ways are called conservatives. Society's "haves" tend to be conservative because they wish to preserve the system that worked well for them.

Although conservatives were in control in 1815, many common people still believed in Enlightenment ideas. People who support new methods for improving society are called liberals. Because society's "have nots" desire change, they tend to be liberal. Liberals are said to be on the political "left," while conservatives are on the political "right." (In the United States the Republican Party is considered more conservative than, and to the right of, the more liberal Democratic Party.) Although the Congress of Vienna succeeded in preventing an outbreak of general warfare in Europe for a century, liberal revolts erupted repeatedly as people continued to seek the Enlightenment goals of freedom and equality.

nationalism

Nationalism is a deep devotion to one's country that places it above all others. It begins with the desire of people who share a common culture to have their own nation free from outside control. In the early 1800s, much of Europe was still divided into small kingdoms often ruled by foreigners. Inspired by nationalism and Enlightenment ideas of freedom, people hungered to belong to their own nations.

In the mid-1800s, most of Italy was ruled by the Austrian and Spanish royal families. There was only one Italian-born monarch, King Victor Emmanuel II of Sardinia. Unification of Italy began here. The king had a clever prime minister named Cavour who helped to unite northern Italy. A popular revolutionary general, Giuseppe Garibaldi, raised an army of a thousand volunteers who brought southern Italy into the Italian union. In 1861, Italy became a nation, and Victor Emmanuel was proclaimed king.

In 1850, Germany was made up of 39 small countries. One of the largest and most powerful was the eastern kingdom of Prussia. Prussia's brilliant prime minister, Otto von Bismark, believed Germany's unification would not be achieved through democratic means, "but by blood and iron." Using a step-by-step approach, Bismark started and won three separate wars against Denmark, Austria, and France, each war bringing him closer to his goal of a greater Germany. By 1870, Germany was unified, and Prussia's king was crowned as kaiser (emperor) over all of Germany. (A prime minister serves as the head of a country's government. In today's world, prime ministers have powers similar to American presidents.)

social Darwinism

In the early 1800s, nationalism was associated with positive ideas like freedom from foreign control. The last half of the century, however, saw the emergence of a darker side of nationalism that glorified war and military conquest. This extreme form of nationalism was supported by racism, a belief that one's own race or culture is superior to others. Racism, in turn, was supported by social Darwinism.

Charles Darwin was an English scientist who had a huge impact on Western thought when he developed a theory of evolution based on the idea of "natural selection." His theory proposed that an animal species may change over time as the best-adapted members survive and the less successful members die out. Social Darwinists took Darwin's theory and used it to justify the racist belief that the world's more technologically advanced white races were fittest and intended by nature to dominate "lesser" races.

The idea of "survival of the fittest" was also adopted by rich industrialists who believed their wealth proved they were superior examples of the human species. Therefore, it was perfectly acceptable for them to enjoy their vast riches while keeping their inferior workers living in poverty.

imperialism

Before the 1800s, Western nations did business in Africa and Asia within existing trade and political networks. After the Industrial Revolution, Western powers used their superior weapons and powerful iron warships to conquer much of the world, especially lands in Africa and Asia. In 1800, Western powers controlled 35 percent of the world's land surface; by 1914, they controlled 84 percent. When a nation dominates or controls another land physically, economically, or politically, it is called imperialism. Western imperialism placed millions of black and brown people under the control of white people.

Imperialism was encouraged by nationalism; European nations wanted to increase their power and pride by adding new colonies. Imperialism was also supported by racist attitudes like social Darwinism. Europeans claimed to be doing "backward" people a favor by conquering their lands and bringing them Western advancements.

But the most important force behind imperialism was money. The Industrial Revolution changed Europe from a consumer of manufactured goods to a producer, and Europe's factories needed places to sell their products. One Englishman said, "There are 40 million naked people [in Africa], and the cotton spinners of Manchester are waiting to clothe them." Colonies provided Europe's factories with new markets for manufactured goods *and* cheap raw materials to feed Europe's machines.

India

From their base in Bengal, the British steadily gained control of India's warring regional states until Britain was master of India. India had the biggest population of any British colony, and it supplied troops to enforce British rule elsewhere in the empire. Soldiers at this time had to bite off the ends of rifle cartridges to load their rifles. When beef fat was used to seal cartridges, Indian troops rebelled because cows are sacred to Hindus. The rebellion quickly spread to other areas of Indian society. After crushing the uprising, the British government took direct control of India from the British East India Company.

India was the "jewel in the crown" of Britain's colonial empire that also included Canada, Australia, and big chunks of Africa. This was the Victorian Age of Queen Victoria, when Britain was at the height of its power.

It was said, "The sun never sets on the British Empire." Britain brought advancements to India including a postal service, telegraph, good roads, and a railroad network. But British control also harmed Indians. For example, the spinning of cotton in Indian homes had long been a source of income for peasants until they were put out of work by inexpensive cotton cloth imported from England's textile mills.

Australia

Australia is the only country that is also a continent. Like the Americas, Australia was settled twice: the first time by hunter-gatherers called Aborigines who arrived by boat from Southeast Asia some 50,000 years ago; the second time by Europeans. The Dutch spotted Australia first, but found it a barren land and lost interest. British explorer James Cook found more promising land in southern Australia and claimed the continent for Britain. The British first used Australia as a prison colony; Australia's first European settlers were convicts. After gold was found in the mid-1800s, European immigration to Australia boomed. The native Aborigines experienced the usual pattern of decline after contact with Western diseases and weapons.

Southeast of Australia lie the islands of New Zealand, where the British subdued native tribes of hunter-gatherers called the Maori (MOW-ree). New Zealand was added to the British Empire in 1840. The British took control of Canada from the French in 1763. Many French-speaking Canadians remain, primarily in the province of Quebec. Canada is the second-largest country in size after Russia, but most of its people live within 100 miles of its border with the United States. Despite their far-flung locations, the former British colonies of Australia, New Zealand, and Canada are considered part of the Western world.

Opium War

In 1800, China was a manufacturing powerhouse, producing one-quarter of the world's goods. It was the wealthiest country on earth. But there was a problem. The British liked their tea, and Britain was sending huge amounts of silver to China in payment for tea and other products. The Chinese, however, had little interest in British goods. This trade imbalance was draining silver from Britain. What to do?

Britain decided to deal drugs. Britain found that Bengal was ideal for growing opium, a highly addictive narcotic. Britain grew opium in India, shipped it to China, and received silver in payment. Although opium use was illegal in China, large segments of the Chinese population became addicted, especially the poor.

Chapter 9 – 1800s: Industrialism and Imperialism

Alarmed that the opium trade was ruining China's society and economy, the Qing emperor pleaded with the British to stop. When they didn't, he ordered the opium trade shut down. After a Qing official seized and destroyed opium from British warehouses, Britain declared war in 1839. With their superior ships and weapons, and with their bombardment of Chinese ports, the British won an easy victory.

Britain forced China to pay the costs of the war and to open new ports to Western ships. China's defeat was humiliating; not only were foreign "barbarians" dictating terms to China and occupying Chinese territory, the war showed how far behind China's technology had fallen. The Qing Empire continued to weaken through the 1800s. It was shaken by major uprisings and defeated in a war with Japan in 1894. A final uprising in 1911 ended the Qing dynasty, and with it over 2,000 years of rule by Chinese dynasties dating back to the First Emperor in 221 BC. The last Chinese emperor was an eight-year-old boy.

Meiji Restoration (MAY-gee)

In Japan of the early 1800s, the Tokugawa Shogunate was still trying to preserve Japan's cultural traditions through measures such as banning firearms and maintaining isolation from foreigners. But there was a problem. The Americans, like the British, believed in free trade even when a country didn't want to trade. In 1853, a squadron of American warships arrived in Japan and threatened bombardment unless Japan opened trade with the United States. At gunpoint, the shogunate agreed. In the political unrest that followed, members of the samurai class armed themselves with surplus weapons from the American Civil War and overthrew the Tokugawa Shogunate. Japan's feudal system with its shogun and regional warlords was replaced by a modern centralized government that granted equal rights to Japanese citizens.

Although the Japanese emperor had long been mainly a ceremonial figure, the samurai restored power to a new emperor named Meiji. Devotion to the god-like emperor became central to Japanese nationalism. The Meiji government sent officials to the West to learn about constitutional governments and new technologies. With help from Western advisers, Japan joined the Industrial Revolution, building railroads, factories, and a modern navy. For the first time, Japan was stronger than its big neighbor China.

Crimean War

In 1854 Britain and France went to war with Russia to stop Russia from gobbling up more territory in the weak Ottoman Empire. Although the war was fought on Russia's doorstep in the Crimea, the more distant Western powers won with better railways, weapons, and navies.

The war was a rude awakening for the Russians. The czar responded by freeing the serfs and giving them land and some education. He hoped these reforms would increase farm and factory production and generate income to help modernize Russia.

At the time of the Crimean War, more soldiers died from infection and disease than from bullets. Britain sent Florence Nightingale to the Crimea to improve conditions in military hospitals, where she managed to reduce death rates from 45 to 5 percent. In the process, she invented modern nursing. This war also saw reporters use the telegraph for the first time to send home news reports from the front. And this war was the setting for Tennyson's famed poem about a soldier's duty, *The Charge of the Light Brigade*: "Theirs not to reason why, Theirs but to do and die: Into the valley of Death Rode the six hundred."

the Scramble for Africa

By the 1870s, the Atlantic slave trade was over, and Africans continued to rule Africa. Europeans controlled only a few port areas. The Ashanti kingdom, for example, was a prosperous trade center on the coast of West Africa, and the powerful Zulu king in southern Africa had an army of 40,000 warriors. But Africa was too tempting for the Europeans to resist. The king of Belgium told a friend, "I mean to miss no chance to get my share of this magnificent African cake." European powers met at a conference in Berlin in 1884 and divided the continent among themselves. The Africans were not invited to attend.

Then the imperialist powers set about the task of defeating African rulers. The Ashanti, Zulus, and others fought back, but in the end spears were no match for guns. In one battle a British force armed with repeating rifles, artillery, and machine guns lost only 48 soldiers while killing more than 10,000 African warriors. Still, conquering the Africans wasn't always easy, and sometimes it took years. In Ethiopia, the Italian army faced African soldiers armed with modern weapons, and Ethiopia kept its independence.

Seven European powers carved Africa into countries with boundaries that often bore little relationship to the cultural groups living there. Europeans took resources from Africa including rubber, gold, and diamonds, and crops including cotton and peanuts. Some colonial governments were harsher than others, but everywhere European whites controlled African blacks. European domination stopped the natural development of Africa in its tracks, nearly destroying African culture in the process.

Mexico

After achieving independence from Spain in 1821, Mexico was briefly a monarchy and then a republic. Mexico's new constitution guaranteed basic rights to Mexican citizens, but it did little to end inequality in Mexican society. A small group of white, upper-class elites continued to exercise political and economic control over millions of poor peasants and indigenous people.

In 1846, the United States went to war with Mexico and took about half of Mexico's territory, a large region extending from Texas to California and north to Wyoming. In the last quarter of the century, Mexico's economy grew as the nation began to industrialize, but little of the new wealth reached Mexico's rural and urban poor.

Much of Latin America followed a similar pattern. After liberal revolts brought independence from Spain, a white upper class maintained control of society much as it had done under Spanish colonial rule. Conservative strongmen came to power to protect upper-class privilege. Liberals might propose reforms, and the poor might revolt, but little would change. In the late 1800s new wealth came to Latin America from increased trade and industrialization, but it was the elites who benefited. Most people continued to work the land as poor peasants. Latin America was a land of very few "haves" and many "have nots."

Spanish-American War

During the 1800s, the United States followed the European pattern of industrialism and imperialism. The U.S. expanded its territory to the Pacific by conquering Native American nations and Mexican armies. Then, in 1898, the U.S. extended its empire overseas. At this time, Cuba and Puerto Rico were the last Spanish colonies left in the Americas, and the U.S. was sympathetic to Cuban rebels fighting for independence. When the U.S. showed its concern by sending the battleship *Maine* to visit Cuba, the ship blew up in Havana harbor, killing 266 American sailors. The U.S. immediately blamed Spain for the explosion—probably mistakenly. With newspaper headlines screaming, "Remember the *Maine*!" the U.S. declared war on Spain.

In a war lasting only four months, the modern American navy easily destroyed two older Spanish fleets. Theodore Roosevelt and his band of "Rough Riders" became heroes after newspapers reported their daring cavalry charge at San Juan Hill in Cuba. With its victory in this "splendid little war," the U.S. acquired Puerto Rico, Guam, and the Philippines from Spain, and Spain lost its standing as a great power.

In the same year, the U.S. took control of Hawaii. America was now a power in the Pacific.

Five years later, Theodore Roosevelt was president of the United States, and he declared the U.S. would take control of any Latin American country that didn't run its government the way the U.S. wanted it to. This arrogant attitude toward Latin America created resentment against the United States that persists to this day.

Westernization

In the 1800s, nations of the non-Western world had to figure out how to deal with a harsh reality: the Western powers were industrialized, wealthy, powerful, and aggressive. Isolation wasn't effective, as the Chinese and Japanese discovered. Fighting back didn't work either, as Native Americans and Zulus learned. Many believed the only way to deal with the West was to become more like the West, in other words, to modernize and industrialize. We saw this occur in Russia, Japan, Latin America, and elsewhere.

Education was one route to Westernization. Bright young people from the colonies studied at European schools and often adopted Western ideas and values. But when non-Western nations tried to industrialize, they faced huge obstacles. Because the Western countries were first to industrialize, they already knew how to produce quality goods efficiently; they already had large urban work forces, and they already controlled world markets. It was difficult for late industrializers to break into the international economic system.

Some questions to consider:

How was Western imperialism dependent on Western industrialism?

What is the difference between patriotism and nationalism?

Who has the best argument: liberals or conservatives?

In today's world, do powerful countries still believe they have the right to control weaker countries?

Chapter 10

1900 to 1950:
World at War

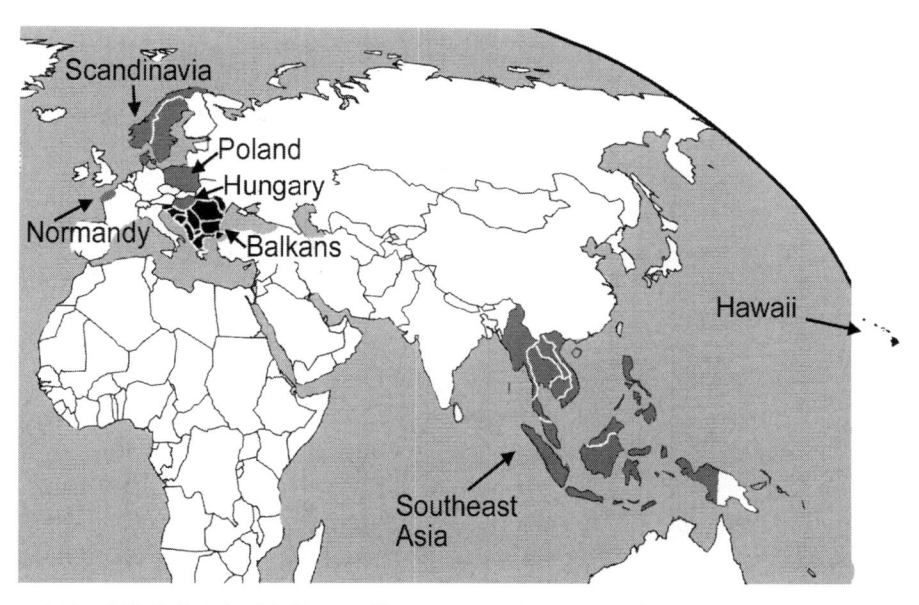

LOCATIONS: The Balkans, Hungary, Poland, Southeast Asia, Hawaii, Normandy, Scandinavia (Locations are depicted on a contemporary political map of the world.)

Preview

At the beginning of the 20th century, Western nations controlled most of the world, and the great powers of Europe were the strongest countries on earth—until they chose to fight each other in two devastating world wars.

Out of the first world war came communism in Russia, Nazism in Germany, and the Great Depression across much of the industrialized world. Out of the second world war came the new military strategy of killing as many civilians as possible, and a terrible new weapon designed for that purpose, the atomic bomb.

the 20th century

Perhaps the biggest change of the 20th century was change itself. In the year 1900, there were no airplanes, televisions, or computers. There were only 50 nations in the world, and only a handful were democracies. A century later, population had tripled. Humans were exploring outer space and surfing the Internet. Empires had dissolved, the world had 180 nations, and most claimed to be democracies. It's been said that more change occurred during the 20th century than in the previous 19 centuries combined.

At the beginning of the 20th century, Europe was at the height of its power, controlling most of the land surface of the earth. The French had built the Suez Canal in Egypt linking Europe to Asia, and Europe's powerful navies patrolled the oceans. Europeans believed in social Darwinism and the superiority of the "white race." They considered their society to be the greatest achievement of civilization and a model for all other peoples to follow. A major chapter in the story of the 20th century is how Europe destroyed its own dominance of the modern world. This gloomy tale begins with World War I.

World War I

At the dawn of the 20th century, Europe's competing nations were as quarrelsome as ever. Nationalism and imperialism increased tensions and conflict among the Great Powers of Europe as they competed for military power and colonial possessions. European countries strengthened their armies and navies and formed alliances so they would have friends in case of war. These entangling alliances meant that a quarrel between any two nations could drag more countries into the conflict. Europe was a powder keg waiting to explode.

The spark that ignited World War I came from the Balkans, a region of many cultures and ethnic groups north of Greece that included the nation of Serbia. In August 1914, a young Serbian nationalist, hoping to trigger an uprising of Serbs living under control of Austria-Hungary, assassinated Archduke Franz Ferdinand, next in line to become Austria's emperor. Austria blamed Serbia for the attack and declared war on Serbia.

Serbia's friend Russia declared war on Austria, and the system of entangling alliances kicked in, trapping Europe in an unstoppable chain of events. Six weeks after the assassination, much of Europe was at war. The alliance led by Russia, France, and Britain was known as the Allies; the alliance of Austria-Hungary, Germany, and the Turkish Ottoman Empire was called the Central Powers. With enemies on both sides, the Central Powers had to fight a war on two fronts.

Chapter 10 – 1900 to 1950: World at War

The fighting in Belgium and France was the Western Front; the war in Russia was the Eastern Front. Patriotic young men from both sides eagerly enlisted for the fight. They expected it to be all over by Christmas.

trench warfare

War had always been a battle of men. The Industrial Revolution turned war into a battle of machines. Five new technologies changed the nature of warfare: the airplane, the tank, the submarine, poison gas, and the machine gun. Of these, the machine gun was the most devastating. At the beginning of the war, generals familiar with an earlier style of combat hurled heroic cavalry and infantry charges against the enemy, but horses and human bodies offered little resistance to machine gun bullets.

As the first winter of the war approached, soldiers on the Western Front began digging hundreds of miles of muddy, rat-infested trenches where they tried to hide from machine guns and exploding artillery shells. Between the trenches lay a no-man's-land of barbed wire, shattered trees, shell craters, and rotting corpses. When ordered to attack, soldiers climbed out of their trenches, ran across no man's land toward the enemy trenches, and were mowed down like fields of wheat by machine gun, rifle, and artillery fire. In just one engagement, the Battle of the Somme in northern France, 1,100,000 soldiers died. Young men were being slaughtered by the hundreds of thousands, and neither side was gaining ground.

the Lusitania

President Woodrow Wilson tried to keep the United States out of the war, but it became increasingly difficult. In 1915, a German submarine sank the British passenger liner Lusitania, which was carrying weapons, as well as passengers, from the United States to England. Of the 1200 people killed in the attack, 128 were Americans, mostly women and children. The sinking turned American public opinion against Germany. Economic interests also pushed America toward war. American banks had made large loans to the Allies, and if the Allies lost the war, these loans might never be repaid. When it looked like the Allies might be defeated, President Wilson took the United States to war.

The United States declared war in 1917 "to make the world safe for democracy," in the words of President Wilson. With a million fresh American troops arriving in France, the Allies soon defeated the Central Powers. When the fighting stopped at 11:00 o'clock on the 11th day of the 11th month, soldiers from both sides came out of their trenches and cheered. November 11th is now observed as Veteran's Day in the U.S.

Treaty of Versailles

The Great War, as it was called, changed the political landscape of Europe. Gone were the Austro-Hungarian Empire and the long-decaying Turkish Ottoman Empire. Their lands were broken up into smaller nations. Russia lost its czar, and Germany's kaiser was replaced by a new German republic. The war nearly wiped out an entire generation of young men in Europe. Almost 30 million people were killed or wounded during the Great War, and over a million civilians died as a result of the fighting.

The peace treaty ending the war between the Allies and Germany was signed at the palace of Versailles in June 1919. Against the wishes of President Wilson, the treaty punished Germany for the war by taking away its overseas possessions and strictly limiting Germany's army and navy. Worse for the Germans, they were forced to make large payments, or reparations, to the Allies for war damages.

The treaty also established the League of Nations, an assembly of sixty countries that agreed to work together for world peace. The League was the idea of President Wilson, who hoped the Great War would be "the war to end all wars." The United States Senate, however, refused to approve the treaty largely because many in America wanted no more foreign entanglements, an attitude called isolationism.

crisis of meaning

The huge numbers of both military and civilian casualties made World War I the first total war. When it was over, people had difficulty making sense of the war. What was the point when the results were weak economies, unemployment, and the destruction of a generation? Historian Pamela Radcliff calls this a "crisis of meaning." How could Europeans continue to consider themselves the most advanced culture in the history of the world when Europe had nearly committed suicide? Colonial peoples wondered what gave Europeans the right to control others if they couldn't control themselves.

People began to see a link between technology and destruction; some questioned if modern technology was such a good thing after all. This crisis of meaning was reflected in Dada and surrealist art movements that attacked basic Western values that went back to the Enlightenment, ideas like progress and the value of human reason. Psychologist Sigmund Freud probed the unconscious mind and found a "human instinct [for] aggression and self-destruction." Freud questioned which side of human nature would win out in the end: the beast-like, emotional, irrational side or the side of reason.

communism

The German philosopher Karl Marx invented modern socialism in the 1800s as a reaction to the working-class poverty of the Industrial Revolution. His slogan was "Workers of the world unite!" Marx predicted that workers in the industrialized nations would one day rise up and overthrow capitalism.

In the early 1900s, Russia was not yet an industrial nation; most of its people were poor peasants working the land. Nonetheless, a group of Russian socialists led by Vladimir Lenin thought Russia was ready for a socialist revolution. Their chance came with World War I. The war didn't go well for Russia. The army was poorly led, poorly fed, and poorly equipped, and eventually it fell apart. When soldiers were ordered to shoot women textile workers rioting for food, the soldiers opened fire on their own officers instead. As rioting spread in Russia, Nicholas II was forced to step down as czar in 1917.

Into this power vacuum stepped Lenin's well-organized political party, the Bolsheviks. Promising peace for soldiers, land for peasants, and better conditions for workers, the Bolsheviks took control of Russia in October 1917 and removed Russia from the war. The term communism has come to mean an extreme form of socialism that blends Marx's economic philosophy with Lenin's ideas about socialist revolution.

Struggling to hold the Bolshevik (or Russian) Revolution together, Lenin executed thousands of Russians suspected of opposing communism. Among those killed were the czar and his family. The communists banned other political parties, took over banks and industries, and set up a secret police. The Russian Empire was renamed the Union of Soviet Socialist Republics, or the Soviet Union for short.

social reform laws

Workers in the industrial nations did not rise up in revolution as Marx predicted; they found other ways to improve their circumstances. Finding strength in numbers, workers formed labor unions and called strikes that shut down factories until owners agreed to better pay and working conditions. When all men got the right to vote (universal male suffrage) by the early 1900s, politicians had to listen to ordinary people. Governments responded by passing social reform laws to improve the lives of workers.

Germany adopted laws that insured workers against accidents and sickness, limited working hours, and provided old-age benefits. British Parliament stopped the employment of children under age nine, and required them to attend free elementary schools.

Britain was first to adopt a workweek of 5 and a half days, giving workers more leisure time to attend theaters, play sports, and ride their newly invented bicycles.

Since the mid-1800s, women in Britain and America had been agitating for equal rights with men. In 1872, for instance, suffragists led by Susan B. Anthony were arrested for illegally voting in a U.S. presidential election. By 1939 women in the U.S. and 31 other countries had won the right to vote.

the Great Depression

The situation for workers worsened again in the 1930s due to a worldwide economic downturn called the Great Depression. Several factors led to the Depression including damage done to European economies by World War I and the U.S. stock market crash of 1929. Businesses closed, farms stopped producing, and banks failed. People lost their jobs and their life savings, and they went hungry.

The Great Depression contributed to the postwar crisis of meaning. Millions of men had died in the trenches of a senseless war, and now it made no sense that millions of strong, healthy men couldn't find jobs to feed their families. The old capitalist system didn't seem to be working anymore; some thought it was about to collapse. Many people, Americans included, looked for a newer approach that would give workers a better break. Some looked to the Soviet Union where communism promised a more equal society. Others looked to Italy and Germany, where strong, nationalistic leaders promised a better future.

fascism

In Italy, a powerful political leader emerged who pledged to end Italy's economic problems and restore Italy to greatness. He was Benito Mussolini, leader of the fascists, a political movement that opposed communism and democracy, but favored violence and war and promoted nationalism and obedience to the state. After taking power, Mussolini modernized Italian agriculture and improved the economy. To strengthen his control over Italy, he made himself dictator, took over the news media, and set up a secret police.

Germany too was looking for a strong leader to end its economic problems. Half of the country's labor force was out of work, and inflation got so bad at one point that it took bags of money to buy a loaf of bread. An inspiring public speaker named Adolf Hitler rose to the leadership of a fascist political party called the Nazis. Hitler told Germans they must reclaim their lost territories and build a new empire in Europe. His nationalist ideas took hold in a Germany that felt humiliated by the Treaty of Versailles. With crowds wildly cheering Hitler in huge parades and rallies, the Nazi Party grew in popularity until it won enough votes in national elections to make Hitler the new German leader.

Hitler quickly moved to revive the Germany economy. In just five years, unemployment fell from six million to almost nothing, and the German standard of living rose. Encouraged by anticommunist businessmen, the German parliament voted to turn over absolute power to Hitler. Thus, Hitler used Germany's democracy to end Germany's democracy. Hitler used his absolute power to ban all political parties except the Nazis and to set up a secret police. His enemies were killed, tortured, or imprisoned.

mass culture

Before the industrial era, people usually experienced their culture alone or in small gatherings. They might read a book or play music with friends. This changed when the Industrial Revolution began to manufacture culture as well as goods. By the late 1800s, mass-produced newspapers were a major cultural force, as thousands of people read the same stories at the same time. Mass culture swelled in the early 20th century as the public flocked to buy movie tickets, radios, and music recordings. Sports teams formed leagues that competed nationally. Such shared experiences helped to create mass national cultures.

Some critics were concerned that people were becoming spectators rather than participants by purchasing cultural experiences instead of making their own. Other critics warned that mass culture could be used to control the public by appealing to emotion rather than reason. This fear was realized in Nazi Germany, where the state took control of radio stations and the film industry, and the government learned to skillfully use propaganda to manipulate the public through emotional appeals to nationalism and racism. (Propaganda is a systematic effort, usually by government, to spread ideas or beliefs.) In Nazi Germany, individual thought was overwhelmed by propaganda and mass public opinion.

totalitarian government

For the first time, mass culture made it possible to reach everyone with the same message and to rally entire nations behind a cause. Hitler and Mussolini rallied the masses of Germany and Italy behind fascist nationalism. The Soviet Union mobilized its masses to support "the worker's revolution."

After Lenin died in 1924, Joseph Stalin took control of the Soviet Union. He convinced Russians it was their duty to industrialize quickly. Stalin also confiscated peasants' farms and combined them into large state-run collective farms. In the process, some ten million peasants died or went to prison camps.

Although communists and fascists had different political philosophies, they used similar methods. Both systems were led by strong, god-like dictators who symbolized the state. Citizens were expected to sacrifice their individuality to the will of the state, and many people were happy to give up personal freedom for a sense of belonging to a great cause.

Both systems eliminated dissent; anyone disagreeing with the government could expect a terrifying visit from the secret police. Because these societies took nearly total control over peoples' lives, they are termed "totalitarian." Unlike liberal democracies, where the state is seen as the servant of the people, the people in totalitarian societies are seen as servants of the state. Authoritarian states are similar, but the term implies somewhat less control by government.

Spanish Civil War
The years between World War I and World War II were a difficult time for democracies all over Europe, as they were challenged by socialism on the left and fascism on the right. Not only were republics overthrown in Italy and Germany, most of the democracies of eastern and central Europe also fell during this period. Shortly before the outbreak of World War II, fascists led by Francisco Franco tried to overthrow the elected republican government in Spain. Volunteers from many countries including the United States (the Abraham Lincoln Brigade) went to fight in Spain on the side of the Spanish Republic.

The fascists, however, were supported by Mussolini and Hitler. Hitler used the opportunity to test his modern German air force, the Luftwaffe, against human targets. A disturbing painting by Pablo Picasso portrays the bombing of defenseless civilians in the Spanish town of Guernica, where 1600 residents were killed by German bombers during three hours of terror.

The attack horrified the world, but it was only a preview of massive terror bombing raids against civilians to come during World War II. After three years of fighting, the fascists succeeded in defeating Spain's republican government. Spain remained under Franco's fascist rule until 1975 when Franco died, and democracy was reestablished in Spain.

the Nanking Massacre

Back in the mid-1800s, the U.S. Navy forced Japan to open its doors to foreign trade. Shortly thereafter, America was distracted by its Civil War, and the U.S. left Japan alone for several years. This gave the Meiji government time to figure out how to respond to the threat of Western power. Japan had a long tradition of borrowing from other cultures, especially China, so it is not surprising that Japan chose to borrow industrialism from the West. With an educated urban workforce, Japan's industrial revolution proceeded rapidly. By the early 1900s, Japan had a modern industrial economy.

In 1905, Japan became the first Asian country to defeat a European power when it overcame Russia in the Russo-Japanese War. Victory gave Japan economic control in parts of Korea and the Manchuria region of China; Japan was now becoming an imperialist power, and the U.S. began to see Japan as a possible rival in the Pacific.

Extreme nationalists came to power in Japan saying that foreign conquest was the only way Japan could get the resources it needed. Japan invaded Manchuria and Southeast Asia, claiming to be liberating Asia from Western imperialism.

When Japanese armies took the Chinese capital of Nanking in 1937, they burned the city and massacred between 100,000 and 300,000 Chinese. In what came to be called "The Rape of Nanking," Japanese soldiers brutally raped some 20,000 Chinese women, then killed them or left them to die.

appeasement

Meanwhile in Europe, Hitler promised Germans he would destroy the Treaty of Versailles, and he began by rebuilding the German army in violation of the treaty. Britain and France complained but did nothing to stop him. In 1936, in violation of the treaty, Hitler sent troops into the Rhineland region on the German-French border. It was a risky move, but Hitler calculated that nobody would stop him, and he was right. Hitler then brought Germany and Austria together in a union also forbidden by the treaty.

England and France were following a policy of appeasement, which means they were giving in to Hitler's demands to avoid conflict and the possibility of another terrible war. As the world watched, Hitler's army grew stronger, and each success made Hitler bolder. Next, he took the German-speaking Sudetenland region in Czechoslovakia, and six months later he conquered the whole country.

In 1939, when Hitler's armies invaded Poland, France and England finally declared war on Germany, and World War II was underway in Europe. The alliance of France and England (later joined by Russia and the U.S.) was called the Allies. Germany and Italy (and later Japan) were the Axis powers. Many historians consider World War II to be a continuation of World War I because the two sides were similar in both wars, and German resentment of the Treaty of Versailles set the stage for the rise of Hitler.

blitzkrieg
To overcome the stalemate of trench warfare, Hitler's military planners developed a new battle tactic called blitzkrieg, or "lightning war." Blitzkrieg meant attacking quickly with a strong force of concentrated troops supported by artillery, tanks, and air power. Hitler's powerful German military used the blitzkrieg to quickly overrun Poland and five more European countries. It took the Germans only seven weeks to circle around a French defensive barrier and conquer the strong nation of France.

With France defeated, Hitler ordered massive bombing attacks against targets in England in preparation for a planned invasion. German bombs pounded London for 57 straight nights. These were dark days for the British people; Prime Minister Winston Churchill told his country, "I have nothing to offer but blood, toil, tears, and sweat." British fighter pilots battled the Luftwaffe in the skies over England, aided by radar that could spot enemy planes approaching the English coast. The Luftwaffe destroyed large areas of British cities, but German aircraft losses became so great that Hitler had to abandon his plan to invade England. Churchill praised British airmen by saying, "Never in the field of human conflict was so much owed by so many to so few." In winning the Battle of Britain, the British dealt Hitler his first major defeat of the war.

World War II
The United States was still at peace. Although America was officially neutral in the war, the U.S. sent so much war material to the European Allies that war production helped pull America out of the Depression. In the Pacific, only one barrier stood in the way of complete Japanese control of Asia: the U.S. Navy's Pacific fleet based at Pearl Harbor, Hawaii. The United States insisted that Japan withdraw from the territories it conquered in China and Southeast Asia, and the U.S. imposed an embargo that stopped the shipment of key resources to Japan, a move the Japanese considered virtually an act of war.

Chapter 10 – 1900 to 1950: World at War

On December 7, 1941, the quiet of a Sunday morning at Pearl Harbor was shattered when carrier-based Japanese warplanes launched a surprise attack on the U.S. fleet. In just 30 minutes, American naval power in the Pacific was crippled. Despite the successful attack, the Japanese commander warned, "I fear we have awakened a sleeping giant."

The next day, President Franklin Roosevelt went before Congress and declared, "December 7th is a date which will live in infamy." The U.S. and Britain declared war on Japan. Germany and Italy declared war on the U.S. Now the war in Europe was linked to the war in the Pacific, creating a truly global world war.

America immediately switched to a war footing. Factories began operating 24-hours a day, seven days a week. Chrysler stopped making cars and started making tanks. As American men were called away to fight, American women went to work in war plants making everything from socks to ships. U.S. war production soon equaled that of Japan, Italy, and Germany combined.

The Pacific Fleet recovered sufficiently from the attack at Pearl Harbor to defeat the Japanese Navy in carrier sea battles in the Coral Sea and at Midway. These victories gave the United States naval supremacy in the Pacific for the remainder of the war. The giant was awake.

the Holocaust

Hitler's empire in Europe stretched from Scandinavia to North Africa, from the Atlantic Ocean to Russia. People in lands conquered by the Nazis were expected to serve the German "master race." "Inferior" people such as Russians and Gypsies were to be enslaved or eliminated. Many teachers and other educated people disappeared. But the Nazis reserved their harshest treatment for the Jews.

Hitler's plan for the Jews was called the "Final Solution," which meant complete extermination of the Jewish people. All over Europe Jews were arrested and sent to concentration camps where they were forced to work or were systematically executed. Hitler diverted so many resources from fighting the war to killing Jews that his mass murder operation eventually contributed to Germany's defeat. Of Europe's eight million Jews, the Nazis succeeded in killing six million, an event that came to be known as the Holocaust. When the world learned about the full extent of Hitler's homicidal madness, the word genocide was invented to describe the intentional and systematic destruction of an entire racial or cultural group.

Hitler's invasion of Russia

Hitler was about to make his biggest mistake of the war, the same mistake made by Napoleon over a century earlier. When Hitler couldn't conquer England, he invaded Russia, which brought the Soviet Union into the war on the side of the Allies. As the Russians retreated, they adopted the same scorched-earth policy used by the czar's soldiers against Napoleon. The turning point in the Russian fighting, and in World War II, came in 1943 at the Battle of Stalingrad, where the Soviets captured an entire German army. The Soviets began to push the Germans back, and from then on Germany started losing the war. The Russians, however, paid a terrible price in World War II, suffering an incredible 23 million dead.

From airfields in England, British and American bombers pounded Germany, wiping out entire cities and killing hundreds of thousands of German civilians. In 1944, the Allies launched the massive Normandy Invasion of France, trapping the Nazis between Allied forces approaching from the west and Russian soldiers closing in from the east. With Russian troops only a few blocks from his underground bunker in Berlin, Adolf Hitler committed suicide in April 1945. Germany surrendered one week later.

Hiroshima

Fierce fighting continued in the Pacific. American troops fought and won savage battles against determined Japanese forces trying desperately to hold strategic islands. American bombers began to strike inside Japan, pulverizing Japanese cities. Japan was on the verge of collapse, but it refused to surrender.

Meanwhile, American scientists had perfected the atomic bomb. Hoping to avoid a costly invasion of the Japanese home islands, President Harry Truman ordered the atomic bomb used against Japan. The first bomb destroyed the city of Hiroshima, where 200,000 people died. Three days later, a second bomb produced similar results in Nagasaki. The next day, Japan asked to end the war. Controversy still surrounds the use of atomic weapons against Japan. Critics say a demonstration of the awesome power of the bomb might have convinced Japan to surrender without using this terrible new weapon against people.

Again, the nature of warfare had changed. Genocide and massive aerial bombing raids had made civilians, not soldiers, the primary targets of war. Of the 50 million people killed in World War II, an estimated two-thirds were civilians. The atomic bomb meant that a future world war might kill everyone.

Chapter 10 – 1900 to 1950: World at War

Some questions to consider:

Do today's politicians try to persuade the public through appeals to emotion?

Was it morally acceptable for the Allies to target civilians in massive bombing raids during World War II?

Was President Truman justified in dropping atom bombs on Japan?

Which will win out in the end: the cruel, beast-like side of human nature or the side of reason?

Chapter 11

1950 to the Present: Cold War and Space Age

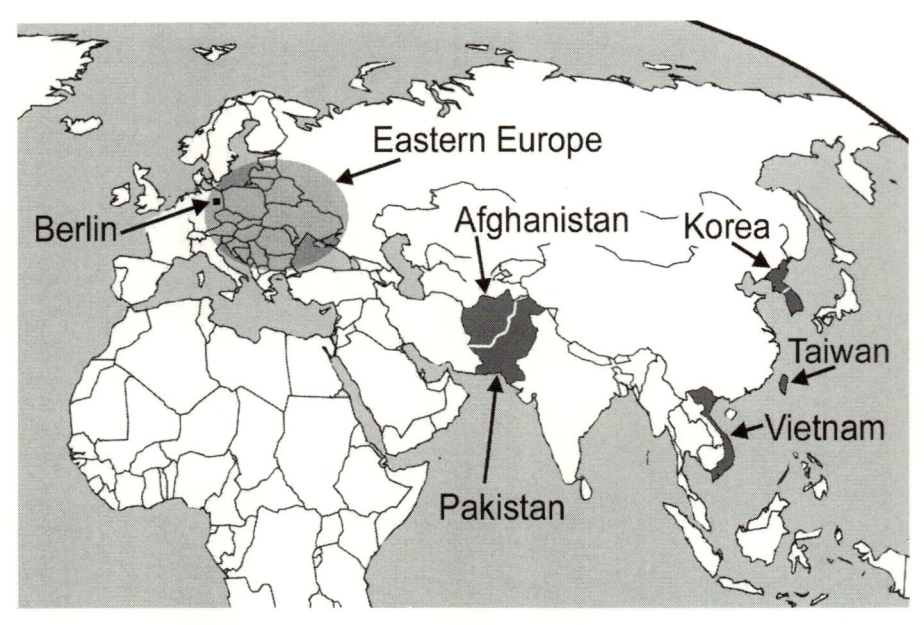

LOCATIONS: Eastern Europe, Berlin, Pakistan, Taiwan, Korea, Vietnam, Afghanistan (Locations are depicted on a contemporary political map of the world.)

Preview

The world was a different place after World War II. Colonialism was no longer acceptable, and Western Europe was no longer the dominant region of the world. It had been replaced by two new "superpowers," the capitalist United States and the communist Soviet Union.

The superpowers would soon be locked in a 45-year political, economic, and military struggle called the Cold War. The superpowers never fought each other directly, but they took sides in "proxy wars" in places like Korea, Vietnam, and Afghanistan. The Cold War led to a nuclear arms race between the superpowers and a space race that sent humans to the moon.

independence movements

Although the 20th century saw human nature at its worst, humans also made great strides during the century. Discoveries in the fields of health and medicine increased life expectancy, and the standard of living rose for people in much of the world. And, following World War II, colonialism came to an end.

Prewar European imperialism was based on the racist belief that the white Western nations were superior to all other cultures, which gave Europeans the right to conquer and control other peoples. After the horrors of Hitler and the Nazis, this kind of racist thinking was no longer acceptable, and the Western powers let their colonies slip away. Some colonies had to fight for independence, while others won their freedom peacefully. Fifteen years after World War II, most former European colonies had gained their independence.

Gandhi

The wave of postwar independence movements began with India, where Indians had been struggling for independence from British rule for decades under the leadership of British-trained lawyer Mohandas Gandhi. Gandhi preached nonviolence; he and his followers were willing to accept pain in their fight for independence, but they were unwilling to inflict it. Adopting a tactic called civil disobedience, they disobeyed unfair British laws, endured police beatings, and went to prison. Gandhi shamed Britain by showing the world that Britain's democratic government was denying democracy to Indians.

Gandhi's independence movement gained widespread popular support shortly after World War I due to the Amritsar massacre, when British troops opened fire on a peaceful gathering of unarmed Indians. The soldiers kept firing until they ran out of ammunition. Some 400 Indian men, women, and children died in the hail of gunfire, and 1200 were wounded. Following World War II, Britain finally granted India its independence, and India was divided into two nations: mostly Hindu India and mostly Muslim Pakistan.

India burst the dam of colonialism, unleashing a flood of independence movements that freed African and Asian nations in the 1950s and 1960s. Gandhi's nonviolent approach was adopted by others including American civil rights leader Martin Luther King Jr. India established a democratic, capitalist system that granted Indians personal freedoms and improved the economy. India became the world's largest democracy, but economic growth did not reach the nation's poor. A huge gap remained between India's prosperous, educated upper classes and millions of poor, illiterate peasants who still lived near starvation.

People's Republic of China

After China's last dynasty, the Qing Dynasty, fell in 1911, China plunged into four decades of turmoil. Following World War II, two Chinese armies fought for control of China. The winners were the Chinese communists, led by Mao Zedong, who established the People's Republic of China in 1949. The losers fled to the island of Taiwan off the coast of China, where they set up an anticommunist government that still exists.

Unlike India's independence movement, which was led by European-trained elites, the communist takeover in China was a peasant revolution. It became a model for peasant revolutions in other places like Vietnam and Cuba. Mao's government made some huge mistakes; an estimated 30 to 50 million Chinese died from starvation when the communists mismanaged the process of setting up large collective farms. But in the end, the communists improved China's agricultural and industrial production.

After Mao's death in 1976, China's leaders opened the economy to capitalist-style, free-market competition. Since then, China's economy has grown rapidly, but China remains an authoritarian state that restricts the rights of its people. Nonetheless, the communist government's promise of equality resulted in better nutrition, education, and medical care than in India.

the Cold War

By fighting two terrible wars in the first half of the 20th century, the great powers of Europe ended their own dominance of the modern world. At the end of the Second World War, two new "superpowers" emerged as the world's strongest nations: the capitalist United States and the communist Soviet Union.

The Soviets angered and frightened the West when they took control of eight Eastern European countries on the Soviet border with Europe. The Soviets wanted a protective barrier in case another Western nation invaded Russia as Hitler had done in the 20th century and Napoleon had done in the 19th. The Soviet Union and its "satellites" came to be known as the Eastern bloc or the Soviet bloc.

The U.S. responded to the Soviet takeover of Eastern Europe with the Marshall Plan, a program that sent billions of dollars in American aid to Western Europe to rebuild economies crippled by war and to strengthen them against communism. This was the beginning of an intense 45-year struggle between the Western capitalist democracies and the totalitarian states of the communist Soviet bloc. It was called the Cold War because the conflict did not turn into a hot, shooting war between the two superpowers.

Berlin

At the end of World War II, the Allies divided defeated Germany into two countries, capitalist West Germany and communist East Germany. Although the German capital of Berlin lay deep inside East Germany, it too was divided. West Berlin was a small island of capitalism surrounded by communist East Germany. In 1948, Soviet leader Joseph Stalin tried to force the Allies out of Berlin by blocking all roads and railways into the city. U.S. president Harry Truman faced a tough decision: should he send tanks to break through the blockade knowing this could trigger World War III, or should he abandon West Berlin?

Truman chose a third course, the Berlin Airlift. Within days, American and British cargo planes were landing in Berlin every few minutes around the clock supplying the needs of the city of two million people. Nearly a year went by before Stalin gave in and ended the blockade. Prompted by the Berlin blockade and fears of Eastern bloc military power, the United States and Western European countries formed a military alliance called the North Atlantic Treaty Organization, or NATO.

The Marshall Plan helped Western Europe return to economic prosperity by the 1950s; now West Germans could own refrigerators and even buy cars. Many Europeans were grateful to the U.S. for coming to their rescue in two world wars and for helping to rebuild their war-torn countries. In much of the world, America stood for liberty and generosity. Conditions were not as good under communism. In 1961, communist officials erected a wall dividing East from West Berlin to prevent East Germans from leaving for a better life in the West. The Berlin Wall became the most prominent symbol of the Cold War.

containment

Communists were now in control of the Soviet Union, China, and Eastern Europe. More people were living under communism than capitalism. The West was genuinely afraid of communist world domination and the downfall of capitalism and democracy. Western leaders feared that if another country fell to communism, more might topple like a row of dominoes: this was called the "domino theory." The U.S. set out to do everything in its power to stop the further spread of communism, a policy called containment.

The containment policy got its first big test in 1950, when communist North Korea, backed by the Soviets, invaded South Korea, which was backed by the U.S. This was also the first big test for the United Nations, an assembly of world nations formed at the end of World War II to promote world peace and cooperation.

With the Soviet Union absent during the vote, the United Nations approved a U.S. resolution to send troops (mostly American) to repel the North Korean invaders. Reluctantly, China was drawn into the war in support of North Korea. After three years of bloody combat, the Korean War ended with North and South Korea occupying much the same territory they held when it began.

Vietnam War

Before World War II, Vietnam was a French colony. During World War II, Vietnamese communists fought Japanese invaders and rescued downed American flyers. After the war, the Vietnamese fought France for independence and won despite American support for France. Although the communists were fighting for freedom from foreign control, U.S. leaders saw Vietnam as a "domino" that must not be allowed to fall to communism. The U.S. set up an anticommunist government in south Vietnam and sent thousands of American military advisers to support it. When it looked like the American-backed government was about to fall in 1965, President Lyndon Johnson took the U.S. to war. Three years later, a half million American troops were in Vietnam, and U.S. warplanes were dropping more bombs than fell during World War II.

Although the two sides were in the same conflict, they were fighting different wars. The U.S. believed it was fighting the spread of international communism; the Vietnamese believed they were fighting for freedom from an imperialist power just as they had fought the Japanese and French. The U.S. found itself bogged down in a guerrilla war with no front lines and few large battles; the enemy would attack and disappear. As the fighting dragged on year after year, and the U.S. death toll mounted, American public opinion turned against the war. With no end in sight, the U.S. withdrew from Vietnam in 1973. A small, poor, rural country had defeated the most powerful nation in the world, and no more dominos fell.

proxy wars

Although the United States and the Soviet Union never fought each other directly, they supported opposing sides in armed conflicts around the world. Local wars like Korea and Vietnam turned into substitutes, or "proxies," for the superpower death-struggle between communism and capitalism. The U.S. backed anticommunist forces everywhere, even dictatorships that overthrew democratically elected governments. Critics of U.S. policy accused America of betraying its democratic principles, but defenders of U.S. foreign policy argued that communism was so evil it had to be opposed by all means possible.

Chapter 11 – 1950 to the Present: Cold War and Space Age   115

The Soviets had their own "Vietnam" experience in a proxy war in Afghanistan, where Soviet troops were sent to fight anticommunist Muslim guerrillas supported by the U.S. The Muslim fighters, who included Osama bin Laden, won with help from shoulder-fired antiaircraft missiles supplied by the United States. Again, guerrilla fighters from a small, poor country had defeated an invading superpower.

nuclear arms race

The United States was the only nation to possess atomic weapons at the end of World War II, but the Soviets soon developed their own atomic bomb. Cold War competition turned into a race to build the most deadly weapons of mass destruction. In 1952, the U.S. detonated the first hydrogen bomb, with a thousand times the power of the bomb dropped on Hiroshima. A year later, the Soviets had the H-Bomb.

Both countries developed long-range missiles that could fly across the earth to deliver nuclear warheads on enemy cities. The superpowers placed nuclear missiles on submarines that could escape detection, lie in wait off the enemy's coast, and wipe out large cities in minutes. The U.S. and the Soviets developed the capacity to destroy each other many times over and to turn the earth into a dead wasteland.

The U.S. placed missiles in Turkey on the Soviet Union's border. The Soviets placed missiles in Cuba, only 90 miles from Florida. During the Cuban Missile Crisis of 1962, the superpowers narrowly avoided World War III when they agreed to remove their missiles from both Cuba and Turkey. Fear of a nuclear holocaust hung over the earth; finally, some weapons had become too terrible to use.

Space Age

The United States and the Soviet Union carried their Cold War rivalry into outer space, competing in a space race closely tied to the arms race; it was long-range missile technology that made space flight possible. The Space Age began in October 1957 when the Soviets launched Sputnik, the first human-made satellite, into Earth orbit. America was caught off-guard and rushed to develop its own space program, which, after many failures, launched satellites into orbit. Then in 1961, the Soviets sent the first man into space. America followed with manned space missions. In 1969, the U.S. overtook Russia in the space race when American astronaut Neil Armstrong became the first human to set foot on the moon, an event that future historians may view as a major turning point in history.

Something unexpected happened when humans left the Earth, and we got our first good look at our home planet. It was a stunning sight!

In contrast to all the lifeless worlds visible in the heavens, Earth was a lovely blue sphere floating in space with white clouds swirling over pinkish continents. In all the dark, lonely, vastness of space, we could see only one water-covered world teeming with life.

We realized how unusual and precious our planet is. This new view of Earth might represent the most profound shift in human perspective since the great voyages of discovery, and it came at a time when that beautiful blue sphere was being threatened with nuclear and environmental devastation by one of its own species.

modern art

After modern art began with Impressionism in the late 1800s, it took off in many directions. Most modern art doesn't look much like the real world, which can make it difficult for people to understand and appreciate. The two main categories of modern art are representational and abstract. Representational art portrays recognizable objects expressed through the artist's personal vision. Abstract art makes no attempt to portray the real world at all, reducing art to its fundamental elements of line, shape, color, and texture.

Reflecting its time in history, much modern art (and literature) has expressed anxiety resulting from two world wars, the threat of nuclear annihilation, and the loss of individuality in mass culture. Pablo Picasso used both representational and abstract styles to convey his horror at the bombing of civilians at Guernica during the Spanish Civil War. Picasso's broken and disturbing images suggest a chaotic world in which principles of morality and decency have been shattered, and civilization is reduced to rubble.

At the middle of the 20th century, art moved toward the abstract, and art could be big and playful. Claes Oldenburg, for example, created huge vinyl hamburgers and a 45-foot steel clothespin. Christo hung a gigantic orange curtain between two Colorado mountains. Many scholars believe the foremost art form of our age is motion pictures, which combine visual images with elements of literature, music, and theater.

collapse of the Soviet Union

In 1985, a new and younger leader, Mikhail Gorbachev, came to power in the Soviet Union. He believed that progress in his huge nation depended on making fundamental changes to the Soviet system. Communism might have sounded good in theory, but it wasn't working very well in practice because people had little incentive to work hard or improve their products. Gorbachev called for a more open, democratic government and economic reforms that looked a lot like capitalism.

He also signed treaties with the U.S. limiting nuclear weapons, and he surprised the world by giving up Soviet control over the satellite countries of Eastern Europe.

In a wave of rebellion, most countries of the Eastern bloc threw off their communist governments in 1989, and Germans happily smashed the Berlin Wall to pieces. Back in the Soviet Union, forces unleashed by Gorbachev's reforms were spinning out of his control: regions of the Soviet Union itself were breaking away and setting up independent republics.

In 1991, the Soviet Union ceased to exist, replaced by 15 new capitalist nations, the largest of which is Russia. Life got worse for many, and several of the republics have found it difficult to establish working democracies and healthy economies. The collapse of the Soviet Union meant the Cold War was over, and there was only one remaining superpower, the United States.

Some questions to consider:

Would Gandhi's nonviolent approach have worked against Hitler?

How did fear on both sides contribute to the Cold War?

Was it acceptable for the U.S. to overthrow democratically elected governments during the Cold War?

Does a stronger country have the right to invade a weaker country to force the weaker country to do what the stronger country wants?

Why were local fighters in the American colonies, in Vietnam, and in Afghanistan able to defeat superpower armies?

Consider the invasions of Europe and Russia by Napoleon and Hitler, the Japanese Empire's invasion of China and Southeast Asia, the United States' invasion of Vietnam, and the Soviet invasion of Afghanistan. Do these events tell us anything about the long-term success of military invasions of distant lands?

Chapter 12

Current Issues:
A Changing World Order

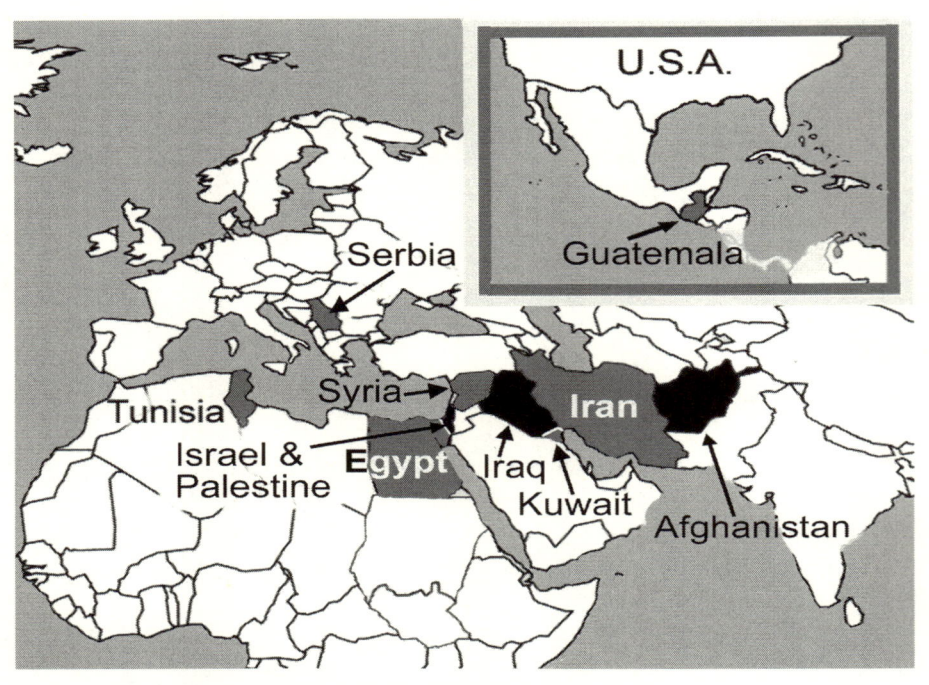

LOCATIONS: Israel, Palestine, Egypt, Guatemala, Iran, Iraq, Kuwait, Serbia, Syria, Tunisia. (Locations are depicted on a contemporary political map of the world.)

Preview

At the beginning of this century, the Cold War was over, and America was the only remaining superpower. The old threat of communism was being replaced by new threats including terrorism and global warming.

While the nations of the world are now more closely linked than ever before by commerce and communication technologies, other technologies have the potential to disrupt life on earth. And many people in the world are still struggling to find enough food to stay alive. Meanwhile, the U.S. became involved in long wars in Iraq and Afghanistan, and China regained its status as a superpower.

Chapter 12 – Current Issues

new world order

At the dawn of the 21st century, the Cold War was over; democracy and capitalism had won. There was no longer a balance of power in the world; America was alone at the top. President George Bush Sr. said there was a "new world order," but history doesn't stand still, and that new order continues to renew. China, for example, has joined the U.S. as a world superpower, and Asia has joined Europe as a global economic center.

One major fear left over from the Cold War is the spread of nuclear weapons, termed "nuclear proliferation." Nine countries are known to have, or believed to have, nuclear weapons—90 percent of these weapons are in the hands of Russia and the U.S. While the United States maintains its large nuclear arsenal, the U.S. has told other nations, particularly North Korea and Iran, that they are not permitted to have nuclear weapons. The United States has not objected to nuclear weapons in the hands of its friends such as Israel, Britain, France, and India. Other members of the nine-nation "nuclear club" are China, Pakistan, and North Korea.

echoes of the Cold War

Two of America's old foes from the Cold War—North Korea and Russia—are again causing problems for the United States.

North Korea, America's enemy in the Korean War of the early 1950s, has been developing nuclear weapons and missiles capable of reaching the United States, which led to an exchange of threats between North Korea's leader and American president Donald Trump. The two leaders later met to discuss the possibility of reducing tensions between the two former enemies by reducing or eliminating North Korea's nuclear program in exchange for economic benefits, but little resulted from these talks.

After the Soviet Union collapsed in 1991, Russia officially became a democracy, but the transition from communism to a free-market economy was difficult, and Russia suffered an economic downturn that might have been worse than America's Great Depression of the 1930s. In the year 2000, Vladimir Putin came to power in Russia, and he led an economic recovery that made him so popular with the Russian people that he has been able to increase his personal power and limit democracy.

Putin has also worked to restore Russia's power and influence among the nations of the world. Concerned that Eastern European countries in Russia's neighborhood were joining NATO—the Western military alliance—Putin pushed back by supporting an invasion that took back the Crimean peninsula, which Russia had granted to Ukraine in 1954. Putin also sent military forces to support Syria's brutal dictatorship during the Syrian civil war, and Putin has been accused of conducting cyber attacks against Western democracies, including the United States.

Iran

In 1951, the government in Iran voted to take control of its oil industry from the British. In response, the U.S. Central Intelligence Agency (spy agency) secretly organized the overthrow of Iran's democratically chosen leader and replaced him with a monarch, the shah. For 25 years, the shah supplied the U.S. with Iranian oil and a base of operations in the Middle East.

But the shah's harsh dictatorship angered many Iranians, and his efforts to Westernize Iran were seen as threats to Muslim culture. Popular uprisings ended in a revolution that overthrew the shah in 1979. The shah was replaced by a radical Muslim government that despised the U.S. for its longtime support of the shah. When the shah arrived in the U.S. for medical treatment, Iranians feared that the U.S. might try to return the shah to power again. Demanding that the shah be turned over to Iran, a group of young Iranian revolutionaries stormed the U.S. embassy in Iran and took 52 Americans hostage for over a year.

(The leader of neighboring Iraq, Saddam Hussein, took advantage of the hostage crisis to attack Iran. The U.S. supported Iraq's invasion of Iran, but when Saddam invaded neighboring Kuwait a decade later, the U.S. quickly crushed Iraq in the Persian Gulf War.)

America still has a difficult relationship with Iran; the U.S. has accused Iran of working to make nuclear weapons, but Iran says it only wants to make peaceful nuclear power. In 2015, Iran agreed to limit its nuclear program in return for the lifting of international sanctions that were crippling the country's economy.

terrorism

The Islamic revolution against the shah in Iran marked the emergence of a new political force, Islamic fundamentalism. Fundamentalists tend to believe that people should adopt basic religious values and that religion should influence government policies. Christian fundamentalism grew in the United States during the same period.

Muslim extremists used Islamic fundamentalism to justify violent acts including the terrorist attacks on September 11, 2001, that killed some 3,000 people at the World Trade Center in New York City and the Pentagon in Washington, D.C. After the attacks, President George W. Bush declared a "war on terrorism" and launched an invasion of Afghanistan, home of al Qaeda, the terrorist organization behind the 9/11 attacks. (Nearly 10 years later, the U.S. located and killed al Qaeda leader, Osama bin Laden.) The invasion of Afghanistan turned out to be the longest war in American history.

While the U.S. war on terrorism was aimed largely at Muslim extremists, terrorism may take other forms as well. In 1995, homegrown American antigovernment terrorists killed 168 people with a truck bomb at the federal building in Oklahoma City. The term terrorism usually refers to attacks against civilians not conducted by a government. When governments attack civilians, they usually call it war or maintaining order.

Iraq

In 2003, the United States invaded Iraq and overthrew the government of President Saddam Hussein. The Bush administration was following a new policy called preemptive war, which means the U.S. may attack a country that has done nothing to threaten or harm America if U.S. leaders feel the country might want to harm America in the future.

President Bush said Iraq had weapons of mass destruction that threatened the U.S., and he indicated that Saddam was involved in the 9/11 terrorist attacks. When it later became clear that neither was true, the Bush administration said the war was still necessary to bring democracy to Iraq. Critics of the war said the U.S. was more interested in controlling Middle Eastern oil supplies.

The United Nations, NATO, and most countries did not support the U.S. invasion. It damaged American relations with important allies like Germany and France, and it turned worldwide Muslim opinion against the United States. The war cost far more in American lives and money than expected, and it triggered deadly violence between ethnic groups in Iraq. It also led to the rise of the so-called Islamic State or ISIS, which took over parts of the Middle East and sponsored terrorist attacks in Europe, the U.S., and elsewhere.

U.S. military forces fought in Iraq for more than eight years, and they were later called back to help defeat ISIS. The U.S. invasion of Iraq resulted in many unintended consequences, much as earlier U.S. interventions had done in Vietnam, Latin America, and Iran.

Arab-Israeli conflict

When the Ottoman Empire dissolved after World War I, Britain took control of much of the Middle East and encouraged Jews to immigrate to their ancient homeland in Palestine, an Arab region at the eastern end of the Mediterranean Sea. After World War II, Britain left the region, and Jews seized over two-thirds of Palestine to form their new nation of Israel. Neighboring Arab countries did not accept Israel's right to these lands and tried to destroy the new Jewish state in a series of wars that stretched from the 1940s to the 1970s. Israel won the wars and took control of all of Palestine.

Israel continues to extend Jewish settlements into Palestinian territory, dismaying those Palestinians who hope to one day reach a permanent peace agreement with Israel.

Arab bitterness has also been directed at the U.S. for playing a key role in establishing the nation of Israel and for strongly supporting Israel since. America faces a difficult balancing act in the Middle East—trying to support democratic and Jewish Israel while staying friendly with authoritarian Arab governments that dislike Israel but support U.S. interests in other ways. Meanwhile, a history of Western imperialism and interventions in the Middle East contributes to Arab resentment against Western nations. Young men and women have been willing to kill and be killed in terrorist attacks aimed at Israel and the West.

the Arab Spring

In the spring of 2011, after more than a century of war and conflict in the Middle East, young people in the Arab world led the way in seeking a better future. First in the north African country of Tunisia, then in Egypt, young people took to the streets in peaceful protests aimed at replacing authoritarian rulers with governments that would grant citizens greater freedom and economic opportunity. The protests grew until the leaders of both countries were forced to leave office.

These "Arab Spring" protests spread to nearby countries including Libya and Syria, where some rulers promised greater freedoms to their people, and some rulers killed protesters in the streets. The Arab Spring left the political situation in the Middle East more unstable than before. Many thousands of civilians were killed—and many thousands of refugees fled—from a terrible civil war in Syria, and Egypt has been placed under authoritarian military rule. Tunisia, where the Arab Spring began, is still working to achieve a more open and democratic society.

ethnic cleansing

Ethnic conflict has been around for a long time, but in 1999 the world recognized a new type of ethnic violence when Serbia was accused of "ethnic cleansing" in the Serbian province of Kosovo. Christian Serbs were brutally forcing Muslims out of Serbia, killing many Muslims in the process.

At the urging of American president Bill Clinton, NATO approved U.S. air strikes against Serbian forces that stopped the ethnic cleansing in Kosovo. Did the U.S. have the right to interfere in the internal affairs of Serbia? Does the world have a moral responsibility to stop atrocities like genocide or ethnic cleansing? Who should decide when war will be waged to enforce morality? Should it be international organizations like the United Nations or NATO or individual countries like the U.S. or Russia?

Latin America

Western nations long dominated the economies of Latin American countries. Latin America followed the classic colonial pattern of exporting food and raw materials in exchange for manufactured goods. These arrangements benefited the white elites who controlled business and government in Latin America but made up less than two percent of the population. Poor, indigenous people received little. The lack of a sizable middle class might help to explain why Latin American economic progress lagged behind that of the U.S. and Canada. Since the late 1990s, however, Latin America has experienced its greatest period of political stability and economic growth since gaining independence in the early 1800s. And its middle class has been growing.

During the Cold War, when local political movements tried to improve conditions for Latin America's poor, the U.S. often labeled these moves as communist threats. In the early 1950s, Guatemala had a democratic government that took unused land from the giant American-owned United Fruit Company and gave the land to peasants. In response, the U.S. arranged the overthrow of Guatemala's government. In the unrest that followed, some 200,000 Guatemalans were killed, many of them poor Mayan Indians.

The United States went on to sponsor the overthrow of governments in several more Latin American countries and acquired a reputation for supporting wealthy elites and military dictators while opposing better living conditions for the poor. In recent years, anti-American leaders came to power in several Latin American countries, promising to use their nations' resources to help the poor—promises that had mixed results.

China

China is again a superpower as it was for centuries before the age of European imperialism. With the world's largest population, labor force, and consumer markets, China's economy has boomed since China opened its markets to capitalist-style competition in the 1980s. Meanwhile, China's one-party communist government continues to deny Chinese citizens basic human rights such as freedom of the press and religion. China shows that a nation does not need a democratic government to have a successful capitalist economy.

Relations between the United States and the People's Republic of China have always been difficult due to their differing political systems, friction over the future of Taiwan, and perhaps because China still resents being pushed around by Western powers during the age of imperialism. Nonetheless, the Chinese and American economies are closely linked. China sells billions of dollars in goods to the United States annually, while the U.S. government has accumulated billions of dollars in debt to China. American officials aren't sure whether to consider China an important trading partner or a possible threat—or both—as China's economy and military grow, and the U.S. and China compete throughout the world for resources, influence, and markets for selling their goods.

Africa

Africa is the world's poorest continent. Unstable governments have slowed Africa's economic progress because foreign businesses have been reluctant to invest their money where conditions are not secure.

During the Scramble for Africa in the late 1800s, the great powers of Europe carved Africa into artificial new countries that included people of various ethnic groups, which the European powers played-off against one another to help them maintain control over people living in the colonies.

When these countries gained independence in the mid-1900s, they had not existed long enough for national feeling to overcome ethnic divisions. Africa's newly independent nations had little or no experience in self-government, yet they had to contend with tough problems like ethnic conflict, poverty, and corruption. Most governments failed.

Ethnic violence remains a problem; it led to genocides in Rwanda and in western Sudan, and it can cause famine by disrupting farming and food distribution. If these troubles weren't enough, Africa was hit with the world's worst epidemic of AIDS.

However, there are positive signs in Africa. White minority rule ended in South Africa in 1994 when Nelson Mandela was elected president in free and open elections, and other authoritarian states have been replaced by more democratic governments. African countries have also made substantial progress in fighting the plague of AIDS.

globalism

The world is being drawn together as never before by international trade, communications, and mass media, a phenomenon termed globalism. Major industries now do business in what amounts to a single global trading market. The labor market has gone global too, as Western companies try to save money and increase profits by outsourcing work to lower-paid foreign workers.

Many people believe globalism is a good thing—that when countries trade and communicate with one another, they are less likely to go to war. In Europe, for example, nations that were bitter enemies during two world wars are now partners in the European Economic Community (EEC), with a common currency called the euro (symbol: €)

Other observers have concerns about globalism. Some say it has made rich people richer at the expense of ordinary workers, and others claim that the wealthy industrialized nations of the world are controlling the global economy, consuming the world's resources, polluting the earth, and leaving little behind for the poorer countries.

capitalism

Although capitalism looked like it had failed during the Great Depression, it survived, and most countries today have capitalist economic systems. To prevent another depression, governments tightened regulation of businesses, banks, and the stock market. Western governments also embraced the economic theories of John Maynard Keynes, who offered an updated version of capitalism.

Unlike Adam Smith, Keynes said government should interfere in the economy. Keynes believed government could stabilize the economy by raising or lowering taxes and government spending. Depressions could be avoided, he said, by increasing government spending, which would create more jobs and increase demand for goods, which would stimulate production. In 2008, the U.S. government successfully used Keynsian methods to prevent a bad economic recession from turning into a depression.

Keynes also advised governments to save for bad times when times are good—something the U.S. government has consistently failed to do. Keynes believed governments would be wise to ease the harshest aspects of capitalism by providing citizens with a "safety net" of programs like Social Security and Medicare to meet basic needs.

In today's global capitalist economy, money flows to countries where wages are lower, which has the effect of gradually leveling incomes across nations. Workers in China are making more money than in the past, while American workers are earning less. Meanwhile, within the U.S., the middle class is shrinking as the income gap grows wider between America's wealthiest citizens and everyone else.

democracy

Although most countries in the world claim to be democracies, true democracy is not easy to achieve or maintain. Democracy appears to work best in societies with traditions of open expression, which might help to explain why democracy has struggled in the republics of the former Soviet Union.

One of the greatest threats facing American democracy today is the huge sums of money needed to win election campaigns.

Because politicians need to raise so much money, they are tempted to make decisions that favor big campaign contributors (such as the wealthy and major industries) over the interests of ordinary Americans. In the early days of the American republic, Thomas Jefferson warned citizens to be vigilant about their government. He said, "The people are the ultimate guardians of their own liberty." Jefferson believed the study of history could help to give American citizens the knowledge they need to think for themselves and to protect their democracy.

A democratic system is effective only if government is being watched by a free and active press and by citizens with a realistic understanding of the world. In America's democracy, citizens can have a big impact; it wasn't government that started the civil rights movement or stopped the Vietnam War. It was the people.

disruptive technologies

Nuclear weapons are not the only technology that has the potential to disrupt life on earth. Biotechnology is a term for technologies that can change how plant or animal life functions. Today, much scientific research is focused on altering genes, the basic units of a person's physical make-up. New gene-based vaccines were developed in record time to control the worldwide Covid-19 pandemic of 2020-21.

One day it may be possible to develop gene-based treatments for nearly every disease, but the same technology could make it possible to alter genes to achieve desired effects such as greater physical beauty, athletic ability, or intelligence. Will people be tempted to alter their children to achieve such results, and is it morally acceptable to engineer human beings in this way?

Other technologies with the potential to disrupt human life include universal digital surveillance that can make it easier for governments to spy on and control their citizens, and artificial intelligence that endows machines with "thinking" powers that could exceed the human ability to control these machines and the unintended consequences of their actions.

the environment

Our last issue may be the biggest. If humans destroy the earth's environment, nothing else matters. Our environment is a complex system of interactions between the atmosphere, weather, chemical compounds, and human activity. Humans appear to be altering this balance through overpopulation and pollution. Most scientists agree that human activity is contributing to global warming, which is changing the earth's climate, producing more wildfires and hurricanes, melting polar ice, raising ocean levels, and causing the extinction of many of earth's species.

Chapter 12 – Current Issues

Although the United States is one of the world's top two polluting nations, it has lagged behind other industrial nations in agreeing to curb the production of greenhouse gasses. These are pollutants such as carbon dioxide from cars and power plants that collect in the atmosphere where they can trap the sun's heat like the glass of a greenhouse.

U.S. leaders have been concerned that limiting greenhouse gasses could hurt American businesses such as the oil and coal industries. Others say that America can help both the planet and the U.S. economy by developing new "green" technologies such as wind and solar power to reduce energy consumption and pollution.

...

What will historians write about America 50 years from now? Will they say the United States was unable to adjust to new realities and declined like other superpowers of the past have done? Or is America exceptional, and future historians will say the U.S. maintained its creativity and kept pace with a changing world? Stay tuned.

Some questions to consider:

What principles and values should the United States stand for?

During the Cold War, was it acceptable for U.S. leaders to secretly overthrow foreign governments without the knowledge of the American people?

Is it true that a democracy needs a free press and informed citizens to function effectively?

Is it reasonable for the U.S. to tell other countries that they can't have nuclear weapons when the U.S. has so many?

Consider the U.S. overthrow of governments in Guatemala, Iran, and Iraq. How do these events illustrate the "law of unintended consequences?"

When is it appropriate for the United States to go to war?

How might our nation's environmental and economic policies be affected by the need of politicians to raise large sums of money for election campaigns?

What did Thomas Jefferson mean when he said, "The people are the ultimate guardians of their own liberty"?

What measures might Americans take to prevent the United States from declining like superpowers of the past have done?

Main Topic Index

20th Century 98
Abbasid Empire 57
Africa (geography) 26
Africa (current) 124
agriculture 20
American Revolution 79
appeasement 105
Arab conquests 54
Arab Spring 122
Arab-Israeli conflict 121
arch (Roman) 44
Ashoka 31
Asia 29
Atlantic slave trade 70
Australia 92
Australopithecus 16
Aztecs 63
BC and AD 13
Berlin (Cold War) 113
Big Bang theory 14
blitzkrieg 106
Bolivar, Simon 83
British Parliament 84
Bronze Age 23
Buddhism 30
Byzantine Empire 50
capitalism (early) 69
capitalism (current) 125
Carthage 42
caste system 29
Catherine the Great 84
Charlemagne 48
China (ancient) 32
China (current) 123
Christianity 48
civilization 21
classical period 47
climate zones 14
Code of Hammurabi 22
Cold War 112
collapse of Soviet Union 116
Columbian Exchange 69
communism 101
Confucius 33
Conquest of Americas 68
conservative vs. liberal 89
Constantine the Great 44
containment 113
continents 15
Counter-Reformation 74
Crimean War 93
crisis of meaning 100
Crusades 58
culture 16
democracy (early) 39
democracy (current) 125
disruptive technologies 126
divine right monarchs 75
echoes of the Cold War 119
Egypt (ancient) 24
Elizabeth I 74
Enlightenment 78
environment, the 126

ethnic cleansing 122
Fall of Rome 45
fascism 102
feudalism 49
First Emperor of China 34
French Revolution 80
Gandhi, Mohandas 111
Germanic tribes 48
globalism 124
Gothic architecture 62
government 25
Great Depression 102
Great Rift Valley 15
great voyages of discovery 64
Great Wall of China 34
Greece (ancient) 38
guilds 61
gunpowder empires 86
Gupta Empire 31
Gutenberg 73
Haiti 82
Han Dynasty 35
Hebrews 23
Hellenistic Civilization 41
hemispheres 13
hieroglyphics (Egypt) 26
Hinduism 30
Hiroshima 108
Hitler's invasion of Russia 108
Holocaust 107
Homo sapiens 17
humanism 40
Hundred Years' War 61
imperialism 91
Impressionism 89
Incas 63
independence movements 111
India (ancient) 29
India (colonial) 91
Industrial Revolution 88
Iran 120
Iraq 121
Iron Age 36
Islam 54
Jericho 20
Julius Caesar 42
Korea and Japan 52
Latin America 123
Lusitania 99
Mali, empire of 57
mandate from heaven 33
Marco Polo 59
mass culture 103
Maya 52
Meiji Restoration 93
Mesopotamia 21
Mexico 95
middle ages 47
Middle East 71
modern art 116
Modern World 68

Mongols 58
Mughal Empire 85
Muhammad 53
Nanking Massacre 105
Napoleon 81
Napoleon's invasion of Russia 83
nationalism 90
Nelson, Horatio 82
Neoclassical art/music 81
New Spain 70
new world order 119
nomadic raiders 32
nuclear arms race 115
Opium War 92
Ottoman Empire 60
Parthenon 39
Pax Romana 43
People's Rep. of China 112
Peter the Great 72
pharaohs 24
plate tectonics 15
primary/secondary sources 12
Protestant Reformation 73
proxy wars 114
pyramids 25
Qing Dynasty 71
Reign of Terror 80
religion 22
Renaissance 62
Roman Empire 41
Roman law 43
Russia (origin of) 50
Sahara Desert 27
samurai 60
Scientific Revolution 76
Scramble for Africa 94
Silk Road 35
Smith, Adam 78
social Darwinism 90
social reform laws 101
socialism 88
Socrates 40
Southeast Asia 51
Space Age 115
Spanish Civil War 104
Spanish-American War 95
Stone Age 17
Swahili Coast 57
Tang Dynasty 51
terrorism 120
Third Estate 79
Tokugawa Shogunate 71
totalitarian govt. 103
Treaty of Versailles 100
trench warfare 99
Vietnam War 114
Vikings 49
Wars of Religion 75
westernization 96
World War I 98
World War II 106
Zheng He voyages 60

Please feel free to email us with suggestions for correcting errors, omissions, and interpretations, or for updating historical material, at contactsf@studentsfriend.com.

Also from Maxwell Learning:

*Future-Focused History Teaching:
Restoring the Power of Historical Learning*

Five basic problems are crippling history education.
We can fix them.

The Student's Friend Concise World History

Designed for classroom and
homeschool teaching.

Available from Amazon and other booksellers.

This book was inspired by the creative mind of Mr. William Teetzel.
Thanks Bill.

Made in the USA
Middletown, DE
05 November 2023